true stories

discover your gifts
find your place
open up to genuine faith

by
Mark Steffey

true stories

ISBN 9798373991506

All Scripture quotations, unless otherwise indicated, are taken from the Holy Bible, New International Version®, NIV®. Copyright © 1973, 1978, 1984, 2011 by Biblica, Inc.™ Used by permission.

Self-published by the author.
Seed funding via Kickstarter.

true stories

Dedicated with love to Kristin

true stories

true stories

true stories

prologue

From my earliest days, my life has been centered around faith. It was, at first, a byproduct of my parents' choices. But as I matured, I eventually claimed a belief of my own. I am not ashamed of this central aspect of how I find meaning in life and I don't shy away from the fact that my view of life has been shaped by my experience of following Jesus.

The chapters you are about to read are not only a recounting of events that have happened throughout my life, but the way in which each event has been interpreted through the lens of my faith journey.

So what's the point?

The point is that some of you might be excited to find out all the different ways that I feel God has been at work in my life and some of you might not be interested in hearing anything about God at all.

Both are great starting points for this book. If faith is not of interest to you, skip over those references. If it is , then I think you will find encouragement in the spiritual connections. Regardless of where you are on the spectrum of belief, each story offers an opportunity to gain insight or wisdom that will help you to make sense of some of your life experiences and hopefully bring enrichment to your relationships, family, work and life.

true stories

My intention in writing this book is to help you reflect on your own journey, to encourage you to think about the events of your life and how they have shaped you, and to reflect on what you have learned from these events about yourself and the world around you.

My hope is that you will see an intersection between your life and God. Or perhaps you have more of a "the universe" philosophy. That's fine too. Either way, I think you will find some truth that will encourage or challenge you.

And that's why I picked the title: True Stories

Stories:
These things actually happened in my life. Some are mundane, some hard to believe, and most somewhere in between. This isn't a book of facts or claims or ideas. It's a collection of life stories.

True:
The details and facts of the stories are recounted as best as I can remember them. A name might be wrong, a date slightly off, or a detail misremembered. But all in all, these things happened as I tell them in the pages that follow.

I don't claim to have a key that unlocks all Truth with a capital T. But I did write down these stories with a purpose. I tried my best to draw out something that rings true about life, the world, and God. I hope that you walk away from each story encouraged, challenged, or comforted. And I hope that you learn, through reading these stories, to reflect on the events of your life so that you can draw meaning from them as well.

OK, that's enough of a setup. Let's get to the stories!

swim team banquet

When you are 11 years old, there is absolutely no logical reason to join a summer swim team. It just doesn't make any sense. First of all, you have to get up early in the morning to go to practice. That's not what summer is for. Summer is for sleeping in, waking up at or after noon, and then sitting on the couch for at least an hour. Get up at the crack of dawn? To go jump in cold water? No thanks.

And then there is the speedo.

As a skinny pre-teen, not even close to puberty, my idea of torture was to be seen by a bunch of middle and high school kids, wearing what amounts to a piece of male lingerie. Again, no thanks.

My younger brother and sister had no such qualms. They loved to swim, and were more than happy to get up early in the morning to join their peers for daily swim team practice at our neighborhood pool.

In my intentional avoidance of all things pool-related, I spent the summer of 1985 focused on something completely different: hip hop. Because of MTV and the growing popularity of urban culture, a suburban white kid like me had a chance to discover and explore this "new" genre of music.

That summer, I listened to as much rap music as I could get my hands on: Run DMC, LL Cool J, Doug E Fresh, and more. I convinced my parents to buy me an Adidas zip-up jacket with three stripes from the shoulder down to the wrist on each sleeve. I had Adidas sneakers with "fat" shoelaces. I was *all* in on my persona as a "b-boy."

But it didn't end with the music and the clothes. There was another important aspect of the hip hop culture that I was committed to: breakdancing.

In the 1980s, breakdancing was the biggest dance craze going, and I would spend hours in my room in front of the mirror, popping and locking and attempting to perfect my style and moves.

I hadn't mastered the difficult breakin' that happened on the floor - the headspins and windmills and arm-spins - but I was fully committed to learning the coolest pops and locks.

While my younger siblings were spending hours at the pool, I was spending hours listening to cassette tapes and dancing in front of the mirror in my bedroom, fully decked out in my Adidas swag.

As the summer progressed I honed my skills to, what I believed, was a high level. When I looked at myself dancing in front of that mirror, I envisioned a crowd of people around me in a big circle, amazed at my moves and cheering me on, "Go Mark! Go Mark!" in rhythm with the beat of the music.

There was one song in particular that had a beat that I was able to really sync with - "The Fat Boys are Back" by the rap group The Fat Boys. I played that song over and over again on my cassette deck, and choreographed a whole popping and locking dance routine, from the first beat drop to the very end.

As June turned to July, and July to August, my popping and locking became more and more fluid. I was sure that if someone watched me dance, they'd be totally impressed.

But when and where would I get a chance to "go public" with my amazing skills?

Summer was quickly fading and with that came the end of the swim team season. This was marked by a celebratory banquet to recognize all of the swimmers' accomplishments.

Of course my parents made me attend, insisting that it was important to support my siblings.

The night of the banquet arrived and I donned my navy blue Adidas jacket and matching shoes with fat laces, along with a pair of white Adidas sweatpants. It was probably 80 degrees out that evening, and I was pretty toasty with long sleeves and sweatpants, but what mattered more was that I looked dope.

The night went on as you'd expect: dinner, awards, speeches by coaches, tributes to the older swimmers in their last season. What happened next was not anything that I expected to be a part of a swim team banquet.

The catering people pushed the buffet tables against a wall, the lights dimmed, and the mom who was the MC for the night got on the mic:

"OK, kids, let's all welcome DJ Mike! Let's have a par-tay!"

Over to the side was indeed DJ Mike, a young guy wearing sunglasses (inside!), standing behind a set of turntables, and flanked on each side by giant speakers. He had a stack of records behind him and with a drop of a needle, the first song came blasting out. It was "Jessie's Girl" by Rick Springfield, a big rock hit back then in the 1980s.

Kids flooded the make-shift dance floor, doing their best versions of dances they'd seen in Footloose or on a Madonna video on MTV. I sat frozen in my chair off to the side.

Song after song blared over the speakers as the DJ played the top hits of the time; Billy Ocean, Phil Collins, Duran Duran, and Katrina and the Waves.

Then, just when I thought the night might be coming to an end, the DJ grabbed the mic,

"Boys and girls, let's groove to the latest trend that's sweeping the country. Here's a track that I know you're gonna dig!"

The next sound I heard gave me chills.

"Fat boys are back, and you know they can never be whack, the fat boys are back, do you lie to the fat boys?"

It wasn't just rap music, it was *my* song.

As I looked around the room at the number of kids trying to do their best breakdancing moves and all looking quite foolish, I knew that it was now or never.

I rose to my feet, zipped my adidas jacket up to my neck, took a couple of steps out on the edge of the dance floor, and started busting out my smooth, slick pop and lock moves. It felt natural. It felt right.

In no less than twenty seconds, a couple of kids near me stopped dancing and started watching me. Then a few more. The next thing I knew, a circle had formed around me, and led by some of the high school kids, the chanting began, "Go Mark! Go Mark!"

I popped. I locked.

And I rocked that dance floor like a real b-boy.

As the Fat Boys song came to an end, I found myself giving high fives to random kids and hearing a chorus of compliments.

"Yo, you were amazing"
"Where did you learn how to do that?"
"That was fresh!"

Covered in sweat and beaming with joy, I walked off the dance floor and grabbed a cup of lemonade. As I sipped from the drink, a smile came across my face. A feeling of real joy. A sensation of bliss. I did it. I had stepped out of my comfort zone and into the spotlight, and I succeeded.

But that was just the beginning. What started out as a personal moment of glory ended up becoming something much more.

I did document that night in my journal as "Personal victory #1" - true story. That night in the summer of 1985 could have just become a cool memory from my tween years.

But it didn't end there. 15 years later, I had the opportunity to speak at a week-long summer camp for middle schoolers. Each night at the all-camp gathering of 250 kids and leaders, there would be singing, skits, and then a message - from me, the camp speaker. I knew that I needed to capture the attention of these energetic 11-to-14 year olds. What could I say or do that would get them focused and listening, not just that first night, but the whole week?

I hatched a plan. A week before the camp, I went to the store and bought a blue zip-up Adidas jacket, just like the one that I wore back in 1985, but an adult medium to fit my current 140-pound 26-year-old frame.

I went to the used record store and found a cassette tape of *The Fat Boys are Back.*

Before the first night's meeting began, I grabbed a guy and girl leader from the camp (who would both be in the audience with their middle schoolers). I told the girl that I was going to tell a story about breakdancing at a swim team banquet when I was 11 years old, and that at the end of the story, she should yell out from the audience, "Do it! Show us your moves!"

I gave the guy the adidas jacket and had him put it on. I told him that after she urged me on, I would say, "Well, I would dance, but there was just something magical about that Adidas jacket."

That would be his cue to stand up and say, "You mean one like this?" He'd then take it off and throw it up to me on stage.

At this point, I'd put the jacket on but tell the audience that I just couldn't do it without that exact song by the Fat Boys. That's when the sound guy would yell from the back of the room, "Good news, Mark, we happen to have that song right here," and hold up the cassette tape that I had given him.

The plan was in place, the night of the first all-camp gathering arrived, and I started out with my story of breakdancing in 1985.

And the audience participation with my "plants" played out seamlessly. It was a huge hit, and once again a room full of people were chanting, "Go Mark! Go Mark!" as I popped and locked on stage in front of the amazed middle schoolers.

But this was different from back in 1985, because it was part of a greater gifting and calling that God had placed in my life, speaking to teenagers and young adults about who He was and how He created them in His image, each of them with their own unique sets of gifts and talents and characteristics. My dancing wasn't simply a talent, it was a means of connection and a part of the purpose of my life.

1 Peter 4:10-11 says,
Each of you should use whatever gift you have received to serve others, as faithful stewards of God's grace in its various forms. If anyone speaks, they should do so as one who speaks the very words of God. If anyone serves, they should do so with the strength God provides, so that in all things God may be praised through Jesus Christ. To him be the glory and the power for ever and ever. Amen.

The word from 1 Peter 4:10 that can easily slip past us is the word "steward". To steward is to look after something, to manage it. A steward on a ship is the person that looks after the passengers and brings them meals.

Imagine that person sitting in the back of the ship's kitchen, carts of meals in front of them ready to be taken around to the passengers, but instead of delivering them, they sit there and feast away, eating and enjoying the food while the passengers stay hungry.

When we keep our gifts and talents to ourselves, or use them only to serve our own purposes, we miss out on the true joy that is found in using them for others.

Discovering my unique gift as an 11-year-old gave me a great sense of personal satisfaction, but using my gift as part of a message at that camp gave me a deeper experience of God-centered stewardship.

And it even multiplied from there. I've ended up telling the breakdancing story and doing the on-stage breakdancing routine as part of my speaking at camps and events all around the country, for middle schoolers, high schoolers, and college students.

I even participated in a local charity fundraiser dance contest (think Dancing With The Stars, without the stars) and won a mirror ball. Yes, you can find it on YouTube.

The gift has been multiplied many times over, in many places, and in a way that actually has little to do with my dancing ability.

It has much more to do with my availability to the calling to use that gift, along with speaking and sharing the hope that I've found in Jesus.

When I was 11 at the swim team banquet, the attention felt good. It gave me a moment of happiness.

But when I tell that story and do that dance in front of a group as part of the telling of a bigger, more significant story of God's purposes for the world, a much deeper satisfaction invades my soul.

What about you? Is there an ability or talent that you possess that could be used to serve a greater purpose? Are there people who could be encouraged, blessed, or even transformed by you turning that gift outward and using it to impact others?

May you discover the way in which God receives the glory when you use your unique talent for His purpose.

true stories

jojo

Growing up in a family where our main activities were sports, traveling, and church, I didn't have much of an appreciation for the arts. As a kid, my parents took us to see the Nutcracker ballet. I mean, they told me they took us, but I think I probably slept through most of it. The closest I ever came to seeing a musical was watching the movie version of "Grease" (my generation's "High School Musical").

My wife Kristin was a college soccer player and also came from a family where sports took up most of the family focus. So when we started our own family, we never even had a conversation about getting our kids involved in the theater. When our daughters were little they took dance classes, but as they got older their natural interests steered them more towards team sports.

Their younger brother Braedan was no different. As soon as he could walk, he started playing sports. He played soccer, baseball, ice hockey, and wrestled throughout elementary school. Somewhere around age seven or eight, Braedan started singing along to songs on the radio. He stunned us with his natural singing voice. Considering that neither of us can really carry a tune, his pitch and tune were remarkable. A few weeks into his 6th grade school year he came home with a flier for the middle school musical, a production called "Seussical", based on the collected works of Dr. Seuss. He said that the chorus teacher was new at the school and that the school hadn't ever done a middle school musical before. The teacher, he said, told him he had to audition. None of our kids had ever auditioned for anything before. The word we knew in our house was "tryout". He was a little apprehensive, but we encouraged him to try something new, so he did. After the cast list was released, he was excited to tell us that he got the role of Jojo. I had no idea what that meant, but he said that it was a pretty big part.

Rehearsals (the theater arts version of "practice") began, and Braedan never went over any spoken lines or singing with us at home. We would inquire about how it was going, and asked if he needed us to help him to practice at home. "Nope," was his only response, and that was that.

We started to get worried...perhaps his role was much smaller than he'd told us. Maybe he was going to learn a good lesson about trying to do something in front of an audience without being properly prepared. Were we about to watch him fail?

About a month later, the night of the opening performance arrived. I asked Kristin how I should dress. I was used to going to the kids sporting events in a t-shirt and shorts, or jeans and a hoodie. She was quick to let me know that it was more of a "business casual" look, even at a middle school musical.

Properly fitted in my khakis and a nice shirt, I arrived at the auditorium and we took our seats in the middle of the venue, about eight rows from the front. Even though it was the first time that the middle school had put on a musical, the place was pretty crowded - it looked like about 300 people. I started to sweat, nervous for Braedan. The lights dimmed, the curtain opened, and then, to my surprise, Braedan emerged, spotlighted alone on the stage. He didn't look nervous. He looked natural, as if the stage was his home. It turns out that

"Jojo" was a main character, and he had several solos and a couple of duets. For the next 90 minutes, I was in total awe. He sang his heart out. He danced with ease and flair. He owned the stage. And he wasn't just good, he was amazing.

I remember turning to Kristin about 30 minutes in and whispering "who is that kid, and where did this gift come from?" About 30 minutes later, as he belted out the last note of one of several solos, I felt tears forming in my eyes. What is happening?! Me, who grew up playing every sport and who had raised kids to compete on the court, field, and ice, had somehow contributed DNA to a person who was totally gifted in an area that I had no (zero, zilch, nada) ability in (other than my amazing breakdancing, of course!)

I'll never forget the audience getting to their feet for a long standing ovation as the cast took their curtain call, and the rise in the volume and shouts when Braedan stepped forward for his bow.

Braedan went on to attend a performing arts high school and majored in Musical Theater. He's been in around a dozen shows, many times as a lead. He even spent a summer as part of the cast of a professional production of, you guessed it...Grease. He shines on stage and dreams of performing on Broadway.

Watching him has taught me that we should never tell someone else what to dream or pursue, and never assume that people around us, even in our families or close circle of friends, are just like us.

Each person has been gifted with a unique mix of God-given abilities and passions. There are as many unique mixes of these gifts as there are people. One gift is not more valuable or important than another. Each one exemplifies God's creativity in the expression of the uniqueness of each individual. And that uniqueness adds color and light to the world.

It's not wise to corner yourself or anyone else into a preconceived idea of what those are or can be.

Ephesians 2:10 says, "For we are God's handiwork, created in Christ Jesus to do good works, which God prepared in advance for us to do."

The word "handiwork" isn't one that we use in day-to-day conversations very much. But it evokes an idea of someone taking their time to make something just as they want it to be. Other translations use the word masterpiece.

You are God's masterpiece, period. He did not mess up. Even if who you are does not fit into the expectations of those around you.

You are 1 in 8 billion.

And you have a unique set of gifts and talents and passions to contribute to the world.

Psalm 139:14 says, "I praise you because I am fearfully and wonderfully made; your works are wonderful, I know that full well."

These words were written by King David, who as a kid was a shepherd on the outside but a warrior on the inside. To his family, he was the scrawny little brother, but God had made him uniquely formed to battle a giant. No one expected anything from young David. Especially not his family. He was essentially an afterthought. But not to God.

Years later, David reflected on this: "your works are wonderful, and I know that full well." You wonder if he was looking in the mirror when these inspired words came to his mind.

Braedan may end up on Broadway, he may end up at a local community theater, or he may end up doing something totally unrelated to performing. Wherever his path leads, I know that if he is sharing his unique set of talents and gifts with others, he will thrive. More importantly, if he is confident in who God made him to be, he will find peace. May it be the same for you!

true stories

nil lara

In the 1990s, there was a traveling summer music festival called HORDE. I know, an odd name. It was an acronym: **h**orizons **o**f **r**ock **d**eveloping **e**verywhere. It was a big deal, and some of the most popular rock groups of the era were a part of it.

When the festival made its stop outside of Pittsburgh, my wife Kristin and I grabbed our sunscreen and blankets and headed out to the amphitheater venue for a day of cool vibes and cold beer.

There was the main stage with the most popular acts and a side stage where lesser-known musicians played. I always like discovering new music, so part way through the day, while Kristin chilled out on the lawn on our blanket, I headed over to the side stage to check out some music.

A sparse crowd was gathered as the next act walked out to start their set. A bald-headed guy led the way, carrying with him a tiny three-stringed guitar-shaped instrument. On his right was a gangly gray-bearded bass player, and behind them, a deeply-tanned tank-topped drummer made his way to his simple kit.

The lead man started strumming the little guitar, and soon the bass and drums kicked in, pounding out a loud, Latin-tinged rock groove. The singer started in on the first verse,

I look around and all I see are politicians on the take
I look at me, I am the same but I don't notice
And I have learned that everybody
Has a price tag on his head
Though it's money that will make the monkey dance

His soulful voice captured my attention right away, and I knew that this was the kind of music that I was going to love.

After the first couple of songs, the singer paused and introduced himself, "Hola, mis amigos, my name is Nil Lara, and this is my band. We are from Miami, Florida."

As they played the rest of their set, the crowd grew in number. Half of the songs were in Spanish, and I didn't understand the words, but it didn't matter. The music and emotions were so powerful and heartfelt. I was hooked.

Over the next year, Nil Lara toured small clubs around the country. I was lucky enough to see him and the band perform twice in Pittsburgh in the mid-1990s. I bought his one self-titled CD and listened to it constantly. I knew all of the words to all of the songs, even the ones in Spanish.

I anticipated that Nil would become a giant star and that I would be one of those people who could claim to be one of the "early fans."

But that didn't happen. Nil Lara and his band eventually ended up back in Miami. He settled down, started a family, and only played occasional local shows in and around South Florida.

true stories

Almost ten years later, my wife and I and our daughters, Hannah (age 2) and Haley (five months old) were vacationing near Fort Myers, Florida. We had flown down from Pittsburgh to see my grandparents and enjoy the Gulf Coast.

Since we were already in Florida, I decided to check in on Nil Lara's website, where he would announce last-second local concerts. To my delight and surprise, the site showed that he was going to be playing at a venue in Coral Gables, the very next night. I quickly opened MapQuest.com and discovered that Coral Gables was less than a 3-hour drive from where we were staying.

I started planning the best strategy to convince Kristin to let me drive down for this concert. Yes, by myself. Yes, leaving her and the girls at the hotel without me. But this my one chance, since Nil had stopped playing anywhere but in South Florida.

First, I phoned the venue, a small bar called The Globe and confirmed that the concert was happening. I asked about tickets, parking, and of course what time was Nil Lara planning to start his set. It was good news: in the Miami area, artists take the stage pretty late. Nil and his band would take the stage at "around 10," I was told.

I mustered up the courage to ask Kristin, and made my case:

I would leave Fort Myers at 6:30, drive straight there, see the concert, and drive back right after, getting back to the hotel by 3 AM at the latest. The only thing I would miss for our girls was the bedtime routine and any feeding of the baby that needed to happen overnight - both tasks that Kristin handled with ease and grace!

27

true stories

Being the amazing person that she is, she agreed!

The next day I was sure to be extra helpful with Hannah and Haley, and when 6:30 finally arrived, I put the pedal to the metal and buzzed down I-75. I didn't even change out of the day's beach attire: a t-shirt, board shorts, and flip-flops.

I arrived at the venue, parked the rental car on the street, and headed into The Globe, which turned out to be a very small bar and music venue in the heart of downtown Coral Gables.

I noticed a couple of things right away:

I was very white. As I looked around, it was clear that the vast ethnic majority of the people in this South Florida club was Latino.

I was not dressed to the standard of the South Florida bar crowd.

My vacation beach look: a t-shirt, board shorts, and flip-flops, was a far cry from the fashion sense of the locals. Almost everyone was wearing a combination of black and white. Sundresses, skirts, white slacks, tight black shirts, and nice, shiny shoes. I stood out like a sore thumb. Or maybe more like a skinny, underdressed white guy.

The Globe had a front section with a lobby and a small bar area, and a back area where there was a series of high and low tables and a simple stage.

I awkwardly made my way over to the bar, pulled up a stool, and sat down. The bartender asked me what I'd like. Most of the people around me were drinking wine or fancy-looking cocktails. I requested a Bud Light draft.

I sipped my beer and glanced around, trying to look relaxed. Was this a mistake? I felt SO out of place. Then a guy sat down next to me, turning to me to start a conversation. As I recall, it went something like this:

"Hey buddy, what's goin on?"

First thing I noticed...he was dressed like me, super casual: jeans, a t-shirt, and flip-flops. I looked more closely and realized: it was Nil Lara!

"Uh...I...it's going great. How are you?"

As Homer Simpson would say: DOH!

"Are you here for the show?" he asked.

"Yes , I am."

The bartender set an open bottle of Stella Artois in front of him.

I am sitting at a bar in Miami, having a casual conversation with my favorite music artist, I thought; this is surreal!

Nil went on, "So where are you from?"

"Pittsburgh," I said as if that's a normal answer.

"Pittsburgh? What the hell are you doing down here, brother?"

"Well, actually I am on vacation in Fort Myers with my wife and daughters, but I drove down here to see, um, well, to see you."

"Really? Truly honored brother. Hey," he turned to the bartender, "his next one is on me."

Nil tipped his bottle to me for a toast. "Cheers, brother."

"Cheers," I said.

"Enjoy the show." He got up, patted me on the back, walked through the bar area, and headed into the back room.

About 30 minutes later, I took my spot along the back wall of the small room where the band had set up. The place held less than 200 people, and it was jam-packed. Mostly couples, 100% locals and 100% sharp-dressed, other than the Pittsburgher in his beach attire.

The band - Nil, his bass player, and drummer - were amazing. They played for a solid two hours, and everyone there danced and sang along to just about every song.

I stood on the back wall, jamming to the afro-Cuban-rock rhythms, lip-synching to the songs that I had been playing on my CD player for almost a decade, including the ones in Spanish.

When it was over, I made the drive back across Florida, fully awake and alert. Still buzzing from the music, I rolled into the hotel at 3 AM.

It was a night that I won't ever forget.

It took a certain amount of extra effort, boldness, and risk.

I had to drive three hours down the coast, then three hours back, in the middle of the night.

I had to walk into a setting where I was dressed wrong and looked totally out of place.

I had to get over whatever silly and misplaced fears that I had about being there.

That's how so many of life's best and most memorable and transformative experiences happen.

We need to learn to step outside of what other people think is normal, even if along the way we make mistakes, don't look right, or feel out of place.

One of the most shocking stories from Jesus' life is recorded in the Gospel of Matthew, where his friend Peter does a very Peter-like thing.

It starts off, though, with Jesus, doing a very Jesus-like thing.

Matthew 25:25-27
Shortly before dawn Jesus went out to them, walking on the lake. When the disciples saw him walking on the lake, they were terrified. "It's a ghost," they said, and cried out in fear. But Jesus immediately said to them: "Take courage! It is I. Don't be afraid."

Jesus is walking on the water! That's not normal. But what happens next is really unexpected. You would think that the disciples would just watch with jaws dropped, and then give him big high fives when he got into the boat. That was probably what most of them were thinking. But not Peter...

Matthew 14:28-33
"Lord, if it's you," Peter replied, "tell me to come to you on the water."
"Come," he said.
Then Peter got down out of the boat, walked on the water and came toward Jesus. But when he saw the wind, he was afraid and, beginning to sink, cried out, "Lord, save me!"
Immediately Jesus reached out his hand and caught him. "You of little faith," he said, "why did you doubt?"
And when they climbed into the boat, the wind died down. Then those who were in the boat worshiped him, saying, "Truly you are the Son of God."

Peter took a risk and put his very life in Jesus' hands.

He seized the moment to turn a cool thing that he was witnessing into a transformational event that he was experiencing.

It didn't go quite as smoothly as Peter might have hoped. He almost drowned. He probably got into that boat with both the admiration of his friends and a little bit of them teasing him as well for almost sinking. But Peter got out of the boat. And for a while, he walked on water. Something no other human has ever been able to claim to have done.

How many times in life do we pass up opportunities not just for memorable events, but for growth and transformation, because we aren't willing to take that step into the unknown?

When we have the opportunity to take risks, we often shrink back because it might be inconvenient, we might look stupid, or we might fail (or in Peter's case, sink). But at that moment, if we are willing to take the risk, we can then and only then experience the reward that lies on the other side.

I am still learning how to do this. I shrink back when I should step out. I often let my fears get the best of me. But I am also finding over and over that when I step out of the boat, God will keep me afloat (hey, that rhymes!). God will meet me and while there may still be some sinking, His hand always guides me back to solid ground.

For me, going to see Nil Lara play in that small nightclub in Florida didn't change my life, but it did teach me the value of stepping out even when it's awkward.

Are you waiting for the exact, perfect setup before taking that risk that you know in your heart is the next step in living your best life? Maybe today is the day you step out, get moving, take a chance. You'll never know what's waiting out there if you stay in the boat. Growth happens when you are uncomfortable. So get going. Great experiences are waiting for you.

true stories

chicken s#!t

I've gotten to see and experience many cool things as I have pursued a life of following Jesus, going to places and meeting people that I wouldn't have otherwise: visited New Orleans to help with relief efforts after Hurricane Katrina, worked with orphans in places like Haiti and Mexico, visited a high security prison in Costa Rica, and had many other amazing adventures. All of these experiences pursued in the name of discovering what God cares about and the desire to come alongside Him in His work.

One of the most amazing times in my life was the spring of 2004, when my wife and I were invited to join a team of about 20 people on a 2-month mission trip to New Zealand. What made it special <u>and</u> challenging was that we took our two daughters with us. Haley was 2, and Hannah actually turned 4 as we flew over the international dateline - May 9 to 11 - skipping her actual birthday (the 10th), which she may someday be grateful for. Like when she can claim to be 39 for an extra year since she didn't actually have her 4th birthday.

New Zealand is a place of great natural beauty, but the people there were the real highlight. We ended up staying in a section outside of the capital city of Auckland. It is predominantly populated by people with a Maori background. The Maori are the original inhabitants of New Zealand and we enjoyed not only learning about their culture, but being immersed in it, from the neighborhood where we walked each day, to the food, and of course the national pastime, the sport of rugby.

However, the trip wasn't exactly meeting our expectations as far as the "service" aspect. Kristin was spending almost all of her time looking after Hannah and Haley. I was able to help out each day at an after-school activities program for a couple of the local primary schools, organizing and running games and teaching lessons, but our vision of serving in some grand way in "missions" had faded.

About three weeks in, the leaders of the trip arranged for us to visit a ministry outside of the city: a working farm that also helped people in drug and alcohol recovery. They had a residency program where men and women would live and work on the farm as they journeyed through their path of sobriety and recovery.

About 15 of us were asked to head out to their facility. We weren't sure what we would be doing to help, but I was sure this was going to be my chance to finally share some of my amazing wisdom with a group of recovering alcoholics and drug addicts.

We arrived at the farm, a sprawling complex of buildings, land, and barns. It was much larger than I had expected. We were greeted by Deb. She was very friendly and definitely in charge. She gave a five-minute overview of everything they had going on at the farm. They had a full produce operation, as well as chickens, dairy cows, a bakery, residential buildings, and more. It was impressive.

She let us know that we'd be breaking up into several groups to help out around the farm. Kristin and the girls went off with a couple of others to help out in the kitchen area, preparing produce that was later to be sold at a local farmers market. One of the older ladies in our group headed to the cafeteria to help set up for lunch. Then Deb asked if our group had any pastors. At the time, I wasn't technically a pastor, but I had been recently employed as a youth pastor, so I raised my hand. Another guy in our group, Sean, was in fact a pastor, so he raised his hand too. "Great," she said, "you two can follow me, I have an important job for you."

This was it. I was finally going to get a chance to speak or teach. I could just picture myself in front of a group, sharing great wisdom and insight. It was about time!

Sean and I followed Deb past a couple of the buildings, back towards the area closer to where it looked like the animals were kept. We stopped next to the chicken coop. It was a big area, with the coop at one end and a large muddy patch, surrounded by a fence. Two shovels were leaning against the fence, along with two sets of work gloves. Next to the shovels was a wheelbarrow.

"OK, Pastor Mark and Pastor Sean. We've got about a week's worth of chicken shit over there in the end building, and we need you to shovel it and take it over to our composting pile in the back."

She pointed to another building, about 50 yards behind where we were standing.

We looked at each other and both tried to fake enthusiasm. Deb handed Sean and me each a shovel.

For the next four hours, we immersed ourselves in this most humbling task. The piles of chicken feces were big, heavy, and smelly.

My vision for what my day was going to look like was altered, to say the least. But as we worked, Sean and I talked. We talked about this place where we were spending the day. We realized that the chickens were laying eggs each day that were either used for food for those living in this community, or sold in local markets to raise money for this ministry. By shoveling and cleaning and adding to the compost pile, we were participating in the transformation of lives.

We then talked about the temptation to view greatness in the way that the world measures it. Those who are in charge. Those with the power. Those with the biggest bank accounts or biggest media following.

We talked about our own temptation to believe in this form of greatness. A temptation that isn't new. After three years of following Jesus, even his closest friends still held onto the world's definition of greatness. Luke, one of Jesus' biographers, wrote it like this:

Luke 22:24-26
A dispute also arose among them as to which of them was considered to be greatest. Jesus said to them, "The kings of the Gentiles lord it over them; and those who exercise authority over them call themselves Benefactors. But you are not to be like that. Instead, the greatest among you should be like the youngest, and the one who rules like the one who serves."

Right before this "dispute", Jesus had instituted the sacrament of communion, explaining to them the way in which he would give up his life, his body and blood, for them. And the next thing they do is argue about who is the greatest!

He reminds them that that is the way the world thinks. The rulers of the world love titles and position. They love power and prestige. But in the upsidedown order of God's Kingdom, service is the way to be great. The first, last. And the last, first.

Does this mean that if we are receiving attention or accolades, we should brush it aside and "play humble"?

Not at all. There are indeed times in life when our skills and gifts and efforts will be noticed by others. That's fine. It's great to celebrate these things. The key is the attitude of the heart. Notice the word that Jesus uses in both instructions to his friends:

"...the greatest among you should be **like** the youngest, and the one who rules **like** the one who serves."

The word in the Greek is "hos". Other places where this word appears it is translated as "as."

It means to embody, to become like, to have the same mindset as. It means saying to God, at every turn, "Here I am, send me."

A few years back I had a chance to speak at a weekend retreat for high school kids. On Sunday, as the event wrapped up, the staff was tearing down the elaborate staging they'd set up for in the main auditorium. I was anxious to get in my car and head home, but not before I collected my payment check from the camp director, Brad. I looked around the room, but didn't see him. Maybe he was outside, saying goodbye to some of the people who'd attended the retreat. I walked outside to where the buses and vans of kids and adults were getting loaded up, but he wasn't out there. I headed back inside, and that's when I saw him. He was 35 feet up, having climbed a ladder, and was helping with the tear down of the decorations around the stage. He was serving. He was sweating. Right alongside college interns.

He was a living example of Jesus' teaching.

Greatness, in the kingdom, means getting up on a ladder at the end of a long weekend. Or picking up a shovel and moving chicken excrement for the day.

What if true greatness means that you pick up a shovel?
What if it means that you lead by example, flipping the structure of hierarchy upside down?

Do you want to be great? Look for opportunities to serve. Get your hands dirty. This is the path to true greatness.

mr. puljos

I ended that last chapter mentioning Brad. Besides directing camps and retreats, he has one of the coolest volunteer positions of anyone that I know. He is the Team Chaplain for not one but two professional sports teams.

Here in Pittsburgh, that's given him the chance to be behind the scenes with MLB's Pittsburgh Pirates and the NHL's Pittsburgh Penguins. He's seen it all up close, from the Pirates three consecutive years making it to the Wild Card round of the playoffs in the early 2010s, to the Penguins' Stanley Cup championship runs in 2016 and 2017.

Being a Team Chaplain for a pro sports team means that Brad has access to the players and coaches, as well as the facilities in which the Pirates and Penguins practice and compete. For the Pirates, it also includes a weekly (optional for the players, staff, and coaches) team chapel service before every Sunday home game. This provides players with an opportunity to grow spiritually during a long season that severely limits their time and ability to attend a local church.

As players arrive at the stadium, Brad sets up in the meeting room right next to the players locker room. About three hours prior to game time, he gets to share a 10-12 minute message to encourage the guys and pass on Biblical wisdom. No singing or prayers or other "church"-type elements. It's very basic, but players appreciate the time to ground themselves in their faith on a weekly basis.

He's been doing this for 20 years, and it's made a big impact in the lives of many players and coaches.

Because I have been working in a similar capacity with college athletes, I am familiar with the format and what is expected. A few years ago Brad gave me a call, asking me if I would be able to fill in for him on a Sunday morning Pirate chapel service while he was going to be out of town.

Of course I said yes.

It was late summer, and the Pirates were in last place in their division. Brad assured me that the mood in the locker room would be loose, and guys were maintaining a positive attitude in spite of their on-field struggles as a team.

He also let me know that part of my duties would be to hold a separate team chapel service for the visiting team. In this case, it was the St. Louis Cardinals. I remember very clearly what he told me next as we talked on the phone earlier in the week:

"After you check in at the Pirates clubhouse, you have to walk through the back hallway to the first base side. That's where the Cardinals locker room is. Across from their locker room is a small meeting room where you will have their Chapel service. You will show the security guard your Guest Pass. He will let you in and then you have to find their Chapel representative, Albert, and let him know when and where the service will be."

"OK," I said, "Albert? Is he one of the assistant coaches?"

Brad laughed, "No, Albert Pujols. The player. He's their chapel rep."

Oh, right. Just stroll into their locker room and walk up to Albert Pujols and chat him up like an old pal. 3-time National League MVP Albert Pujols. As of this writing, #30 on ESPN's list of the 100 Greatest Baseball Players of All-Time. 702 career home runs. That Albert Pujols. No problem.

Sunday morning arrived, and I headed to PNC Park, ready with a well-prepared 10-minute message to share with the Pirates and Cardinals. I got checked in through security and was handed my "Guest Chaplain" pass. I went straight into the Pirates locker room and found the room where I would be leading their chapel.

All of a sudden, I started to get really nervous, and my mind started to do what people call "stinkin thinkin."

Mark, you didn't make it past little league. These guys are pros. They don't want to hear from you.

Really, Mark, you think these rich pro athletes are going to listen to you?

You are 35, and these are young, talented baseball players. They are going to take one look at your 5'9", 145-pound frame and brush you off.

I tried to set those thoughts aside, and then suddenly remembered what I had to do next: go to the Cardinals locker room and talk to Albert Pujols. More stinkin thinkin.

You don't belong in the same room with the great Albert Pujols. What could you possibly have to offer someone like that?

But I had no choice. I had to do my job. I walked down the back hallway, finding my way to the visitors locker room, where I showed my Guest Chaplain Pass to the security guard at the entrance. He opened the door, and let me know that the players area was just down the short hallway, past the visiting Managers office.

I walked in, and started down the hallway, passing by to see Cardinals manager Tony Larusa sitting at a desk in the small office, along with a couple of assistant coaches.

I entered the players area of the locker room. A few players sat on folding chairs in front of their lockers, while a couple of others were planted on a couch at the far end, watching ESPN on a large TV.

I scanned the room. Over on the left, standing with his back to me, was Albert, all 6'3" of him.

The thoughts of inferiority started to creep back into my head, but I pushed them away. I couldn't just stand there. It was time to act.

On the inside, I was incredibly nervous, and the baseball fan in me was kind of freaking out. I was about to not just have a conversation with Albert Pujols, but a conversation where I, in essence, would be telling him what to do. But I had to play it cool. I had to believe that I was legitimately there and belonged. I had to overcome my insecurities and silly thoughts and get on with it.

I walked across the room, then spoke up, trying to sound as confident as I possibly could.

true stories

"Mr. Pujols?"

He turned around. Before he could say anything, I stuck out my hand for a handshake. His giant hand reciprocated, and I stiffened my arm and hand in an attempt to seem super manly.

"I'm Mark Steffey, and I am subbing for Brad Henderson today as the Pirates Team Chaplain. Brad told me that you were the man to talk to about chapel."

"Good to meet you, Mark. Yes, that's me. Sorry to hear that Brad can't be here today. Will the chapel service be in the same place as usual?"

"Yes," I replied, "In the conference room across the hallway. What time do you think will work?"

He looked at his phone, "How about 11:15? Does that sound good?"

"Yes, 11:15 will be perfect," I confirmed.

"Sounds good. I'll let the guys know. See you then. Looking forward to hearing a good word."

I walked out of the locker room a little taller as my insecurity faded and my confidence and sense of self-assurance rose to the surface.

The rest of the morning was awesome. Both chapel services were well-attended, and I could tell that my message connected with all of the players and coaches. I walked out of PNC Park that day having learned a valuable lesson...

true stories

At some point in life, you will be in front of someone who intimidates you or whom you admire. That's the time to be bold, go for it, and let the chips fall where they may.

Throughout my life, this pattern has repeated itself over and over. Just a year later, I was asked to help run a youth football clinic where the Pittsburgh Steelers would be volunteering. My job was to gather the players together, split them up into groups, and get them out onto the field to run the "stations" where the kids would be practicing their football skills.

I literally found myself on the side of the field before the event started with 25 pro football players huddled around me in a circle (including future Hall of Famer Troy Polumalu) as I provided instructions where to go and what to do.

In the years since, I have had the chance to be in front of the New York Mets, Seattle Seahawks, Cincinnati Bengals, Notre Dame football, and more. In each instance, I had to believe that I belonged and that I had something of value to say to the group of men in front of me. My security can't come from how qualified or unqualified they may perceive me to be. I have had to walk into each venue with an attitude of "I belong here" and "I am going to bring added value to this group of people."

All of us will have moments when the opportunity or moment at first seems to be "too big" and we feel insecure. This is true of many people throughout human history, and there are also many examples of this in the Christian scriptures.

One of my favorites is in the Hebrew Bible (what Christians call the Old Testament). It's found in the strange story of Esther and Mordacai. If you have time, try to read all of Esther. It's wild. Oddly, God isn't even mentioned in the whole book.

What is mentioned is the ways in which Mordacai and especially Esther step up and speak up to an intimidating authority figure. I could try to summarize her full story here, but I will cut to the chase. The pinnacle of her life happens when she has a chance to speak up boldly before a king who is planning to kill her family and tribe, and she steps out with courage. She takes action, even though she could be killed. As she is about to take this bold step, she says:

"After that I will go to the king, though it is against the law; and if I perish, I perish" - Esther 4:16

Her bold words are received and the whole plot of the story flips, all because she summons the courage to speak with boldness to a person in authority. I love that she says, "If I perish (die), I perish (die)." She knows the importance of her message is greater than even her own life.

You may not ever stand before a king or a Hall of Fame athlete, but there will come a time when you have your chance to speak up with boldness to that person or group of people that scares you. Don't shrink back. Take a deep breath, realize that you were made for that moment, and speak up.

true stories

dream job

"DaDaDa, DaDaDa"

If you grew up in the peak era of ESPN's SportsCenter, you just read that like I would. It's the unmistakable sound that is most associated with the show, the abbreviated ending of the popular SportCenter theme that was first introduced in 1989.

Like many people back in the 1990s, I was a SportsCenter addict. Forget about the 11 o'clock news. In our house, that time was reserved to watch Keith Olberman and Dan Patrick's deft and entertaining delivery of sports highlights.

This was the age before instant score updates and highlights on your phone, so SportsCenter was the one-stop shop to catch up on the sporting events of the day.

Even into my late 20s, I watched almost every night. One night in the summer of 2003, at the first commercial break, they showed a promo for an upcoming new reality show called Dream Job. The premise was simple. ESPN would be holding auditions around the country to find the next SportsCenter anchor. Sports meets American Idol.

The idea was pretty cool, and of course thousands of men and women from around the country were sitting at home thinking, "I bet I could do that!"

I was definitely one of those people.

But with two small daughters at home and a busy job, I didn't think my wife would be in favor of me auditioning for a sports reality TV show. So I didn't think much about it after seeing that first commercial.

About a week later Kristin and I were driving somewhere. She was reading the sports section of the newspaper, because she is cool like that. A full-page ad for the ESPN Dream Job caught her eye: local auditions were being held at a sports bar in downtown Pittsburgh.

She turned to me, "You should do this. You'd be good at it."

That's all that I needed to hear. We got home, and I called the number on the ad and signed up. A couple of weeks later, I drove down to the sports bar, not knowing what to expect.

I arrived early on a Saturday morning and got in line with hundreds of other people, all waiting for our turn to be seen and assessed, hoping to become America's next great sportscaster. I had nothing prepared and no idea what the audition would entail.

The casting and production staff were bringing in people in groups of 8-10. I noticed that some of the contestants were only inside for ten minutes or so, and then were released, while others seemed to be staying longer.

Finally, it was my turn. I was brought inside the building along with others near me in the line. They sat us along the actual bar and passed out a packet. It was a 50-question sports trivia quiz. We were told that we had 10 minutes to complete it.

I started the quiz. The first few questions were easy. So were the next few. I glanced at other people in my group, and their perplexed faces showed that at least a few of them were struggling. After five minutes, I completed my quiz, confident that I got almost every question correct.

The ten minutes concluded, and a production assistant walked around and collected the quizzes. We were escorted to a nearby table to await the next step in the audition.

A little while later, another staff person announced to our group that only four of us would be moving on to the next round. As she read the names, I was not at all surprised to hear my name called.

The next phase had the four remaining contestants from our group standing around a pool table. A local TV sports guy was there, a legit TV cameraman, and 1970s Pittsburgh Steeler champion Andy Russell.

They pointed the video camera at us and let us know that we had two minutes to come up with a 30-second play-by-play of what we considered the greatest moment in sports history.

I pondered what I would say. Something Pittsburgh-sports related? The miracle on ice? Jesse Owens at the Olympics?

The first guy took his turn, and fumbled his way through the 1960 Bill Mazeroski home run to clinch the Pittsburgh Pirates World Series win over the Yankees. The next guy was an Indiana basketball fan, so he recapped the 1987 NCAA championship-winning basket by Keith Smart.

Then it was my turn.

"Here we are folks at the Penn Hebron Elementary School baseball field. Today's little league game between the Red Sox and Pirates comes down to this. Bottom of the sixth inning, Red Sox at the plate with two outs, down 3-2, with the tying run on second base and the winning run on first. Here's the pitch...and it's a long fly ball to left-center field. This one looks to be heading to the gap. But Mark Steffey, the center fielder, got a great jump on that ball! He is on his horse and dives, full extension, and makes an incredible game-winning catch. The Pirates win this one and Steffey's teammates mob him as he runs into the infield."

The local TV sports guy nodded his head in approval.

"You're Mark Steffey, I assume?"

"Yep." I replied with confidence.

"And that highlight is the greatest moment in sports history?" he asked.

"Well," I explained, "for me, it was, because I was there. I did it. So to me, that makes it the greatest."

"Interesting. You're the first contestant who has incorporated themself into their highlight."

The last guy took his turn, recounting the Michael Jordan championship-winning basket against the Utah Jazz, and then we were all instructed to wait at another table for further instructions.

20 minutes later, yet another production assistant walked over to our table.

"Mark Steffey?" she asked.

I raised my hand, and she signaled for me to follow her. We paused after just a few steps and she turned back to the other guys, "Thanks for your time. You all can head out now."

I followed her back into another room, where I was seated at a table to fill out a form: personal information along with a couple of short answer questions about what makes a great SportsCenter anchor.

After I finished, I was instructed that I would be called if I was chosen to move on to the next round.

I left that day feeling pretty good, and the next week I did indeed get that call.

The guy on the phone said that they had more than 15,000 people at auditions around the country. He said that it was very competitive, and that 200 people were being chosen to participate in the next phase. Fifty people in one of four cities: Los Angeles, Atlanta, Chicago, and New York.

"Congratulations, Mark. You are one of three people from our Pittsburgh audition who have been selected. Your next step will take place in New York City at the ESPNZone at Times Square this coming weekend. You are responsible for getting there and your accommodations. You need to be ready to go, onsite, Saturday morning at 8 AM."

I hung up the phone and was pumped. 200 out of 15,000? Not much more than 1%! That's something to be proud of! But now it was going to cost me: transportation to and from New York

City, plus a hotel room. Oh, and at the time I didn't even own a suit, so there was that too!

I bought my first suit (at age 29), an Amtrak train ticket, and booked a room at a hotel close to Times Square.

Friday arrived and I was on my way.

After the long train ride, I finally arrived at Grand Central Station, walked to the hotel, and checked in. The room was about the size of a large closet and cost a ridiculous amount of money, but it was just a short walk to where the next stage of the audition would take place the following day.

I got up early Saturday morning, put on my new suit, and headed to the ESPNZone. After checking in, I was directed to a conference room, where the other 49 contestants and I would spend what turned out to be a very long day.

We were interviewed by ESPN staff, filled out more surveys, and each took a turn showing off our anchoring skills in front of the producers, including Al Jaffe, the network's Vice President of Talent.

Finally, in the late afternoon, they gave us a two-hour break. We were instructed to be back by 6 PM for the reveal of the 12 people who would be moving onto the next round of auditions.

The ESPNZone was located on the corner of 42nd Street and Broadway, right in the heart of Times Square. Most of our time had been spent on the first floor of the building. At the beginning of our break, I took an escalator up to the second floor. There I found an open space and big windows overlooking the intersection below. I was by myself and it was quiet. The streets below me were bustling with thousands of people moving about under the New York City lights; some shopping, or headed home from work, or there to visit the sights of the Big Apple.

As I observed the scene, I felt God speak to me in the depths of my soul. It wasn't an audible voice, but it was a voice nonetheless. He allowed me to see the people below through His eyes. What did they need? What was my part of that? Did God need or want me to be a guy reading sports highlights to them on TV? Was it His ultimate purpose and desire for me to become a SportsCenter anchor?

I knew in my heart what He was saying to me to answer those questions. The Dream Job might be someone else's calling or purpose, but I knew at that moment that it wasn't mine.

"Mark, people like the ones you see on the streets below, they need me. And your calling is to be a person who tells them about my love."

I took a deep breath and allowed myself to believe that word, which seemed as clear to me as anything that I'd ever known or experienced.

At the end of the break we were all gathered in the conference room, where the cameras rolled as ESPN's Linda Cohn announced those chosen to move onto the next round of the contest. My name wasn't called.

It was confirmation that God had brought me there, not to get my dream job, but to remind me of the unique calling He places in each person's life.

The journey to New York City for the audition did have a purpose, even though it wasn't what I had expected.

That's how life often works.

A tangent, a detour, an exploration of something outside of our "normal", ends up being a turning point or a moment of clarification and confirmation of some other direction or calling or purpose.

My calling was clarified as I looked at a crowd of strangers on the streets of Manhattan.

For me, it was the beginning of a transition into a long season of life where my main focus wouldn't be reading sports highlights, but would be investing in student athletes and sharing with them the story of Jesus.

The missionary to the non-Jews, Paul, wrote a long letter to the Jesus followers in Rome, and in part of it he reminds them that each person brings a unique set of gifts to the world:

Romans 12:4-8
[4] For just as each of us has one body with many members, and these members do not all have the same function, [5] so in Christ we, though many, form one body, and each member belongs to all the others. [6] We have different gifts, according to the grace given to each of us. If your gift is prophesying, then prophesy in accordance with your faith; [7] if it is serving, then serve; if it is teaching, then teach; [8] if it is to encourage, then give encouragement; if it is giving, then give generously; if it is to lead, do it diligently; if it is to show mercy, do it cheerfully.

true stories

These words are written to people within the very specific context of a church community in the 1st century, but the guidance rings true on a much wider scope.

We all have different gifts. Find the ones that are yours, and don't follow someone else's dream.

I love sports.
I love people.
I love telling people about Jesus.
I am young at heart.

This mixture has led me to a vocation that brings those strengths together in a way that I would have never planned on my own, but it somehow has worked out just as God intended all along.

What about you? Are you chasing down the "dream job," even though it doesn't fit with who you know you are created to be? Or are you seeking to combine your gifts and skills with a God-directed purpose?

Dream Job aired on ESPN that spring, and I appeared on screen for precisely one second on the first episode. But in the 20 years since then, my gifts and talents have taken me on a journey that I wouldn't trade for anything.

true stories

futbol en las montañas

It was a picture-perfect day in the rural mountain village a few miles outside of the southern Mexico city of Tepic.

I stood on the mostly dirt soccer field awaiting the referee's whistle to begin the game. I was excited. I was nervous. I was ready.

No, I wasn't there as part of a journey through the Mexican futbol leagues to become the next Messi or Ronaldo.

I was there as a 27-year-old youth pastor who had retired from organized soccer at the age of 13. I'd brought a group of high school players to serve the community, play games, be immersed in the culture, and build community. The boys that I brought were all ages 15 to 17, and two of their dads had come along as well. Neither of the dad-chaperones were soccer worthy, so I had to step in and become the 11th man.

I wasn't totally out of shape, but I wasn't in "soccer" shape and it had been 14 years since my last action. I had volunteered to play defense but had proven to be a liability. My lack of skill and below average fitness made me ineffective as a midfielder.

The team determined that the best place to "hide" me and my ineptitude was at forward, playing alongside our best attacking player, Ian. My job was to run around and be a decoy, drawing the attention of the other team's defense so that we could give Ian time and space with the ball.

We'd spent the first few days playing soccer games closer to the city. Our hosts had arranged these exhibitions, and after each game both teams would gather, along with anyone who was there to watch, and we would share about our faith, pray for everyone, and hand out snacks.

Now our hosts had loaded us into a bus and taken us more than two hours into the countryside, up narrow, winding roads, to a remote village. Our next soccer game was about to begin.

The locals were prepared to play and a young, intimidating squad stood at the ready across the midfield line.

As the game began, dark, ominous clouds appeared to the east just over the top of the nearby mountains. If we had been back in the U.S., this would have been the point at which the game was paused for a weather delay. Not so in rural Mexico. The clouds soon opened up and it poured giant raindrops for the next 20 minutes. But the game continued.

The play went back and forth, and both teams had a hard time controlling the ball on the now muddy and uneven field. I did my job, running around in the offensive half, trying to give Ian as much space as possible, when and if he received the ball.

As quickly as the storm had arrived, it stopped. The sky turned blue and the clouds disappeared. Now the sun was shining above us, but the mud and slush remained.

Right before halftime, our Mexican opponents won a direct kick right outside of the penalty area. The captain of their team stepped up and rocketed a free kick into the top corner of the goal, giving them a 1-0 advantage.

It remained 1-0 into the second half of the game. I was a complete non-factor, but I was pretty tired from all of my "decoy" running.

As we approached the end of the game, the referee looked at his watch and signaled there were only a couple of minutes remaining. I figured that I should use the rest of my energy up, so I made a run to the wide right side of the field. As I hoped, a defender followed me, leaving space for our central midfielder to play a perfect pass to Ian as he streaked diagonally across the center of the pitch. He took one deft touch past the defense, pivoted inside to his stronger right foot, and blasted a shot. As the ball headed for the upper corner of the goal, the goalie leapt and managed to tip the ball over the crossbar, giving our team a corner kick and one last chance to tie the game.

Our whole team came forward, including our goalie, hovering around the 18-yard-box as we waited for the corner kick to be taken by another one of our best players, Matt.

I lingered at the far side, trying to stay unnoticed by the other team. A couple of them glanced at me and then decided to mark other players on our team, realizing that I was the least likely person to get on the end of the oncoming corner kick.

Matt raised his arm to signal that he was ready. He booted an inswinging ball into the box. The curved trajectory sent it rapidly towards the crowd of players near the goal.

I moved closer to the far post, and my depth perception quickly alerted me to the fact that the ball was headed my way. With no defender within five or six feet of me, I knew what I had to do. I dove forward towards the flight of the ball, attempting to time my leap to strike the ball with my head to send it into the back of the net for the game-winning goal.

Time slowed down. The ball struck my forehead just perfectly as I closed my eyes, my body now suspended in the air horizontally like Superman in flight.

I felt the impact of the ball, then the impact of the ground as I landed face first in a puddle of mud at the edge of the goal. I stood up, ready to be embraced by my teammates for my late-game heroics.

Pushing myself up from the ground, I looked to see if the ball had nestled into the back of the net.

Nope.

The ball had struck my forehead, but what I hoped would happen didn't. The ball had flown high over the goal, and the other team's goalie was now racing to retrieve it for a goal kick.

No, I didn't score the game-winning goal.

Yes, my face was covered in mud.

The other team rushed forward as our team retreated. The goalie blasted a long goal-kick up the field. An opposing player ran onto the ball and shot a rocket from nearly 40 yards as our goalie, who'd been at the other end of the field attempting to help us score on the corner kick, frantically ran back, flailing at the shot, only to see it bounce perfectly into our goal. 2-0.

true stories

I watched this last chain of events unfold as I wiped mud away from my eyes, nearly 100 yards away, still getting to my feet after my failed attempted header.

I wasn't the hero. I didn't have my moment of glory. In fact, at the moment of opportunity, I fell flat on my face.

And that's the end of the story.

No great moment of redemption in our next game.

That was it.

Done.

Failure is a part of life. Falling flat on your face sometimes is followed up by...nothing.

On this journey we call life there are going to be memorable stories of personal triumph, moments of epiphany, and clear glimpses behind the curtain to see the grand design of it all.

But not always. Not in every event. That day, on that soccer field, at the moment of possible greatness, I failed.

Yes, believe that someday I will see how all of my failures and foibles were woven together as part of some great redemptive purpose.

That day will come. But it's not here quite yet. In the real world, on this side of eternity, some failures just feel like failures.

The true stories of people from the Bible can help us gain this eternal perspective, but that is because we have the benefit of hindsight. I bet that it didn't always feel like that to the people who lived through those failures.

The first humans didn't trust God, and gave into the temptation of the forbidden fruit. (Genesis 2)

One of their kids murdered the other. (Genesis 4)

Noah got drunk and fell asleep naked. (Genesis 9)

Abraham didn't fully trust God's promise and took a naughty shortcut. (Genesis 16)

Lot offered his daughters up for sex. (Genesis 19)

We aren't even out of the first 19 chapters of Genesis.

Did God weave all of these failures together into a purposeful plan of ultimate redemption? Yes.

Did it seem like it at the time? No way.

Sometimes we fall flat on our face. No lesson, no moment of redemption. For my soccer playing, that was it. There's nothing more to the story. I failed. We lost. Turn the page, move on.

I remember that day on the soccer field and how I came up short in my possible moment of glory. And for the life of me I have tried to find some great lesson in it. Nada. Zilch.

For every event that has happened in my life where I have been able to later see the way that it had some purpose, either in the short term or long term, there are a bunch of things that have happened where that isn't the case.

I bet the same is true for you. And that's OK.

Today, if you fall face-first into that puddle of mud, it may be to teach you some lesson. Or it may just be a puddle of mud. Move on. Keep going. Don't allow defeat to define you and don't stay stuck in the moment of misery.

true stories

little death hollow

Spring Break.

For most college students, those two words bring to mind sandy beaches, tanned bodies, and plenty of alcohol. But in 1994, when I was a sophomore in college, it meant a one-week backcountry hiking trip in the canyons of Utah. Our college campus minister, Sandie, who loved the outdoors, convinced (coerced?) a group of us to pile into a couple of 15-passenger vans and head out west. The diverse group was made up of guys and girls, freshmen through seniors, experts, and novices. We all signed up based mostly on her enthusiastic sales pitch about how amazing of an experience the trip would be. It also helped that Sandie had spent months, and in some cases years, caring about each of the participants as a friend and mentor. We trusted her because she'd shown us love and spent time investing in our lives: attending sporting events, taking us out to coffee or lunch, and taking an interest in the things we cared about.

This was pre-Google-Maps, but Sandie had done the research and came up with six days of hiking that would challenge us and take us deep into the backcountry of the Utah canyons.

After the loooong drive from Ohio to Utah, we found our way to a small parking lot at a trailhead somewhere in the middle of nowhere. We set up camp for the night and prepared for six days of strenuous, real hiking and camping. We'd be leaving the vans there and going into the heart of the canyon, with only the supplies we could carry in our (very) heavy backpacks.

Things went smoothly for the first couple of days. We'd hike, stop to eat and get hydrated, and then hike some more. Each evening we found a flat, open space to set up camp. On day four, Sandie informed us that our trek that day was going to take us into a remote area of the canyons to a place called "Little Death Hollow." Really, that's the name. Back then we couldn't Google it, but you can now. Go ahead.

As our hike continued through the day, the tall cliffs of sandstone on both sides of us grew closer and closer together until they were only a few feet apart. This is known as a "slot canyon," because as you hike through it feels like you are indeed in a slot between two giant walls of rock. Our group of 15 marveled as we hiked one hour, then two, then three through the increasingly narrow trail. It was really cool. Until it wasn't.

As the afternoon shifted towards evening, we encountered an area about five feet wide, filled with water that was about four feet deep. Fifty feet ahead, two large boulders blocked the canyon, rising five to six feet above the water. Adding to the situation was the fact that the base of the canyon received little or no sunlight, making the muddy pool's temperature sitting somewhere just above freezing. It seemed, for a moment, like we had two choices: turn back, or figure out a way forward. However, we quickly realized that turning back would more than likely lead to us not making it out of the slot canyon before dark, setting up camp in the canyon was unwise, due to the possibility of flash flooding.

Sandie and our other leaders, Dave and Tricia, huddled together for a quick decision-making meeting. They then announced their plan to the group. As we heard their idea, we trusted that they knew best. Sandie had been a guide and mentor to almost everyone in the group throughout our college era, so that deposit of trust made her leadership easier to follow.

The choice was made, and it was clear that turning back was not an option. We had to go forward, in spite of the obstacle in our way.

But there was another challenge. The four days of hiking had taken their toll on our team. Steve, a big guy who was a tight end on the football team, and Justin, the starting goalie on the soccer team. had both come down with a stomach bug that had zapped them of their strength. These two capable guys were down and out.

With Steve and Justin out of commission, others had to step up. Jen, a soccer player and a very quiet member of the group, took on a role of active leadership in this tough moment, not by anything she said, but through her actions.

The biggest two guys in the group, Dan and Jeff, walked through the deep water first, holding their backpacks above their heads, then heaving them up over the wedged boulders. Next, Jen went through, climbing over the boulders with a boost from the first two guys. Then, one by one the rest of us went through. The three-person team at the boulder-end would lift and assist each person over the boulders. One girl, Monica, was too short to go on her own, so she hopped on the shoulders of someone else as they walked through.

The greatest challenge was still ahead, as we had to figure out a way to get our fallen pair, Steve and Justin, over the boulder. Jen offered up an idea: she'd get back into the ice-cold water and boost them from below while Dan and Jeff pulled them from on top of the boulder. Without hesitation, she jumped back in the frigid water. It was so inspiring to see her step in and help, even at the expense of her own comfort and safety.

Finally, everyone was through, other than Jen. We worked together to reach over the boulders and pull her up and over to safety. Exhausted and freezing, everyone took a few minutes to rest and warm up before continuing on our hike. We were eager to make it to a safe place and set up camp.

I took a moment to look back at the place from where we had just come, shaking my head, somewhat amazed that we made it through. It then occurred to me that if it was just one of us, or even two of us, who had encountered the water and boulders, we wouldn't have been able to get through. It was working together, relying on and trusting each other, that enabled us to make it past the obstacle.

Obstacles are a part of everyone's journey through life. Sometimes they are small and easy to get over, and other times they seem impossible to conquer. There are times we can see them from a distance, and other times they appear out of nowhere. When we face them, a mistake we often make is to face them alone.

God has placed people in our lives for us to lean on, rely on, and work with to overcome almost any obstacle.

Ecclesiastes 4:9-12 says
Two are better than one because they have a good reward for their toil. For if they fall, one will lift up his fellow. But woe to him who is alone when he falls and has not another to lift him up! Again, if two lie together, they keep warm, but how can one keep warm alone? And though a man might prevail against one who is alone, two will withstand him; a threefold cord is not quickly broken.

We live in an age of isolation. Many people struggle to make it through life's muddy waters, often because they are facing their obstacles alone. What we need to realize is that we aren't meant to go it alone. We are made to live our lives surrounded by people we can lean on and people who can lean on us.

If you find yourself alone as you face your next trial, have the courage to reach out for help. There are people who would be blessed by knowing that they can be the friend that you can lean on. The help you need may come from an unexpected source. Like Jen on the hiking trip in Utah, there are people in our midst who will surprise us with the support and boost that we need, if we are willing to accept their help.

The next time you find something seemingly impassable in your life, don't turn back. Find a trusted, caring leader. Lock arms with two or three people, and share the burden of the obstacle with them. Then work together to make it over.

true stories

3 v 3, but also 5 v 13

One of the best things about living in Pittsburgh is that our professional sports teams have had plenty of success over the years. OK, the Pirates are a bit of an exception, but six Super Bowl trophies and five Stanley Cups is pretty darn good. For a relatively small city, we have been spoiled.

Pittsburgh's NHL team, the Penguins, hit the draft lottery twice over the past 30 years. Each time they were able to select a generational talent. First, in the 1980s, it was Mario Lemeiux. His leadership brought two championships to the Steel City. Then, in the 1990s, Sidney Crosby, who led the team to three more Cups. During both of those eras, the region saw a big increase in the number of kids playing ice hockey.

Neither Kristin nor I played ice hockey growing up. So when Haley, our middle child at the time, expressed a desire to try it, we figured it would probably be a short-term thing. Boy, were we wrong! As a six-year-old, she stepped on the ice and was a natural. She skated with grace, speed, and flawless technique. She breezed through the different levels of the required skating classes, and within a couple of months we had signed her up for the Mini Mite House League for kids six years old and younger.

Out of more than 80 kids, she was the only girl. But her ponytail wasn't the only thing that stood out. Her natural skating skills, effort, and excellent hockey sense were very impressive.

A couple of years later, she tried out for her first travel boys team, and made the AA Mite team. Again, she was the only girl, not just on the team, but in the league. Her team won the playoffs that season and she scored the go-ahead goal in the championship game.

Braedan and Hannah also got the hockey bug, and both ended up playing AA and AAA hockey (the highest youth level) over the years.

But hockey is really Haley's thing. She's played all over the country and in Canada, made National Development Camp twice, and ended up playing hockey in college.

Over time, I have evolved as a hockey dad. I started out as a crazy hockey dad. You know, the yelling, over-involved, wacky parent in the stands. That was me. But over the years I have reformed into a laid-back, quiet fan of my kids.

I have only coached my kids a few times, and one time with Haley was an epic experience.

It was summer 3v3 at our local rink. This is the time of year when the seriousness of travel hockey is replaced by "fun" full-ice 3v3. The rules are adjusted to increase scoring and give kids a chance to try fancy moves. Rather than traditional line changes (players coming on and off of the ice within the natural flow of the game), this 3v3 format includes a buzzer every 45 seconds. At the sound of the buzzer, the three players on the ice leave the puck wherever it is and skate to the bench, and three new players jump onto the ice.

The other big rule change from regular 5v5 hockey involves penalties. In "real" hockey, most penalties result in a player having to sit in the penalty box for 2 minutes, so their team has to play "short-handed" until that time expires or the team with the "power play" scores a goal. But not so in 3v3. In 3v3 every penalty is a penalty shot. Trip an opponent: penalty shot. Touch the puck after the buzzer sounded at the end of your 45-second shift: penalty shot. Mouth off to the refs: penalty shot.

The role of "coach" in this scenario is basically just to stand behind the bench and make sure that kids are getting enough water between shifts, and in the case of nine and ten year olds, to open and close the bench doors, since they aren't big enough to hop over the boards.

But this summer league had playoffs, and of course kids (and dad coaches) always take playoffs seriously.

Haley's team was called the Rockets. Like always, she was the only girl on the team. There were four teams that made the playoffs, and the Rockets were the 3rd-seeded team.

The thing about 3v3 summer hockey is that by the time the playoffs hit in late July, families are on vacation, kids are away at summer camps, or there are other sports conflicts like summer tournament baseball. So you never know who will show up for the games.

The semi-finals and final were over one weekend, a Saturday and Sunday, in late July. As the coach, I sent out an email to check our players' availability for the games. The replies back were not encouraging. Out of our roster of 14 skaters, only seven were able to play in the semifinals. Even worse, two of those players were leaving right after the game for vacation, so in the event that we won and advanced to the final, we would have just five skaters. Thankfully, our goalie, who happened to be one of our best players, would be available for both days.

I wasn't sure if we would be able to win the semi final game, but just out of curiosity I called the league director and asked him what would happen if we won and only had five skaters for the final. He reminded me of the rule which coaches had been informed of at the beginning of the summer: with just five skaters, one of the three skaters on the ice would have to complete their 45-second shift, skate over and tap their stick on the boards near our bench, and then skate another 45-second shift. It's simple, he said: the player would just have to "tag up."

If you don't know much about hockey, here's something to keep in mind. A player who skates up and down the ice for 45-seconds and gives full effort is gassed! It's like sprinting for 45 seconds, but even tougher, because you are engaging your whole body while also balancing on two blades that are each one-eighth of an inch thick! Skating back-to-back 45-second shifts is not easy, to say the least.

Heading into Saturday's game against the #2 seed, I secretly hoped we would lose and avoid the final. After all, we would likely be playing the #1 seed, who had beaten us all three times that we had faced them during the regular season.

Our seven skaters and excellent goalie showed up on Saturday morning for the semi-final. I could tell in the locker room that they were ready to go, and the fun of the summer regular season was replaced by a serious tone. At nine and ten years old, kids want to win, even if the only prize is a "3v3 Champions" t-shirt.

Another dad, Ryan, joined me behind the bench to help coach our squad. The semi-final ended up being pretty lopsided, in our favor! From the opening puck drop, our kids were flying, working together as a team and skating hard every shift. The game was three 15-minute periods, meaning that with seven skaters, everyone was on the ice a lot. At the end of the first period we led 4-1, at the end of two it was 6-3. Even with a short bench, we pulled away in the third period and won the game 12-6. Haley had a hat trick (three goals), including a slick top-shelf backhand goal after dangling around two defenders.

As the final buzzer sounded, the team celebrated and headed for the locker room. Ryan and I walked behind them, and he turned to me and said. "Well, at least we made it to the final."

The next morning when I woke Haley up for the game, she told me she was excited and ready to go. I didn't want to spoil her optimism, but in my mind I was thinking, there is no possible way that we can beat the #1 seed with just five skaters.

We arrived at the rink and the kids got ready - all six of them - five skaters and the goalie. There was plenty of space in the locker room that day! I gave the kids a couple important pieces of game strategy. First, stay hydrated. Each player would be playing at least 60% of the game, so when you come to the bench, get water right away. Second, with the rule about "tagging up", I explained that it was important to keep a mental note of the time left on each 45-second shift, and that whichever player was closest to our bench would be the one to tap their stick and tag up, as long as they hadn't already been on the ice for two consecutive shifts. It was a lot for the kids to handle, but I told them to do their best and have fun.

As the players got on the ice for warm ups, I noticed two things about the opponents (the team that had defeated us three times over the last month):
1. There were 14 skaters, so they would have much more energy than us.
2. They were all goofing around during the warm ups, laughing at the fact that we only had five skaters.

I called our team over to the bench. I said, "Look at the other team. They are laughing. They aren't taking this seriously. They think the game is already over. Let's give them a dose of Rockets reality!"

The game started and the play went back and forth. Haley and her teammates played with grit and teamwork. They followed our "tag up" plan to perfection. At times it even worked in our favor because the player who was tagging up was right next to our bench at the end of the 45-second shift, meaning that they had a bit of a head start, rather than having to come off of the bench to start their shift.

As coaches, we were doing a lot more than just standing behind the bench. We had to have water bottles ready, had to yell for which kid should stay on the ice, and remind them of how much time was left at the end of each shift.

Amazingly, the game was tied at the end of the first period 2-2, thanks mainly to the stellar play of our goalie, who had to have made at least 20 saves, including several on clear breakaways.

The second period was just as tight, and I could see our players getting more and more tired. As the buzzer sounded to end the period, the other team scored a last-second goal to take a 5-4 lead heading to the third and final period.

Our kids came to the bench. I was so proud of them, but I could tell from their faces that they were exhausted. I reminded them that there was no game tomorrow or the next day or even the next week, so it was time to leave it all on the ice. They all nodded their heads in agreement.

Play in the third period was intense. The other team started skipping the shifts of some of their less-skilled players. Even though they had 14 skaters, only eight or nine were getting time on the ice. Like I said, teams took winning those "3v3 Champions" t-shirts very seriously. Even if it meant giving less playing time to a 9-year-old.

As time was winding down, we were trailing 6-4. With less than two minutes remaining, Haley darted through the defense and rocketed a shot off the bottom of the cross bar and into the goal to pull us within a goal, 6-5.

The kids only had a couple of minutes of hockey left, and I thought, well, there is nothing wrong with losing a game by one goal when you only have five skaters for a 3v3 game!

Then it happened. Our best player, Carter, was fighting for the puck along the boards when an opposing player tripped him from behind with his stick. The ref raised his hand and called the penalty, giving Carter a penalty shot with just under one minute remaining.

The ref placed the puck at center ice and Carter skated towards it, grabbed it with the blade of his stick and maneuvered towards the goal. He faked a shot and the goalie bit, leaving the top of the goal wide open for him to flip the puck into the net. Tied 6-6!

Meanwhile, the other team's coach was going berserk, yelling at the official for the tripping penalty. The ref had had enough. He signaled a "T" at the coach, giving him a bench minor penalty, and awarding us yet another penalty shot!

By this time the clock had wound down to zero, so this final penalty shot would either give us the victory or send the game to overtime. And in the case of a penalty on their coach, it was up to us to decide which of our players would take the penalty shot.

I called the kids over to the bench, and asked them who should take it. They all pointed at Carter.

"OK, Carter, you got this," I said.

The rink fell silent. Carter once again skated with the puck, tapping it forward towards the goalie. He went with the same move as in his previous attempt, but this time the goalie stayed up, and slid to his right. With that, Carter deftly guided the puck along the ice between the goalie's legs (the five-hole) and into the back of the net.

Our players rushed onto the ice and tackled him in a pile of celebration. Against all odds, five skaters had done what seemed impossible. They had won the game by believing, working together, following a simple strategy, and never giving up.

We were outnumbered, but not outworked.

Even Ryan and I, on the bench, played a crucial role with our hydration and shift management tasks. You are probably reading this and at least beginning to guess what the lesson to be learned was through this experience. The easy thing would be to go in the "David vs Goliath" route, or maybe another example within the story of the scripture where the underdog, greatly outnumbered, won the battle.

Yes, these are obvious examples of winning against all odds. But the odds aren't what is important about this scenario, or even about those Biblical examples.

I believe that the hockey game taught me lessons about two other important areas: strategy and teamwork.

We had just five players. We had to come up with a system, a strategy, that would be workable based on the situation that we were in. The timing of the players getting on and off of the ice at the beginning of each shift, based on the factors of who was where on the ice and who had most recently already "double-shifted", had to be planned and executed with precision and good communication. Not an easy task for two dads with little coaching experience and a group of young kids!

It reminds me of the earliest followers of Jesus, who were just a small group of men and women within the large city of Jerusalem. They were small in number, but not in faith. They had a variety of gifts and passions, and God enabled them to work together to share the incredible news of the resurrection with the culture around them.

They weren't perfect, and they encountered many challenges, both internal and external. We tend to have a picture of the people in the Bible as two-dimensional figures, but they were actually just people like you and me. As they attempted to proclaim the resurrection of Jesus, complications always seemed to come up. One of the most interesting examples is found in Acts 6. Apparently, the early followers of Jesus had a food distribution system in place to help people who were in need, but for reasons that aren't clear, there were some people being neglected. And while the early leaders were focused on telling others about Jesus, they also realized the importance of taking care of their community. So they worked together to come up with a solution.

The twelve apostles made a statement.

Acts 6:3-6 says,
"Therefore, friends, select from among yourselves seven men of good standing, full of the Spirit and of wisdom, whom we may appoint to this task, while we, for our part, will devote ourselves to prayer and to serving the word." What they said pleased the whole community, and they chose Stephen, a man full of faith and the Holy Spirit, together with Philip, Prochorus, Nicanor, Timon, Parmenas, and Nicolaus, a proselyte of Antioch. They had these men stand before the apostles, who prayed and laid their hands on them."

This may seem like a strange thing to be included in the "holy" scriptures. But they realized that it was just as important to help the needy as it was to preach the risen Jesus. Like in our hockey game, they came up with a strategy, and used a team to get the task done.

The task of distributing food was deemed to be holy. Notice that it says that Stephen was "a man full of faith and the Holy Spirit" and that the apostles "prayed and laid their hands on them." For this specific undertaking, they came up with the right team and the right plan to get things back on track.

82

What about you, in whatever challenge you are faced with in life right now? Do you have a strategy to confront it? Do you have a team around you that is committed to tackling the problem?

I know that in my life it's been a recurring pattern that I have seen play out over and over, in both good and bad ways. At times, I've tried to push forward alone, without a plan, and it has led to failure. Other times, by God's grace, I have had the people and the plan, ready to face and overcome adversity. Typically, I have found more success with the latter.

Whether it's five little hockey players taking on fifteen, or a bigger challenge within a family, at work or school, or within a community, the smart move is to link up with a team and commit together to implement a strategy.

true stories

the accidental half marathon

George Steffey is one amazing guy. He is also my dad. He's been a great role model for me in so many ways: as a man, as a husband, as a father, and as a follower of Jesus.

Back in 2012, right after he turned 70, he shared with me one of his goals for the year: to run his first marathon before he turned 71. He'd run a few 5K races, and was pretty fit for a man of his age. He looked much younger than his years, something that could probably be attributed to, in part, his fitness.

But there is a big difference between a 5K and a marathon. A 5K is 3.1 miles and a marathon is 26.2 miles. That's quite a jump. And a 70-year-old running a marathon for the first time? Not very common!

I was excited for him and wanted to lend him whatever encouragement and support that I could. So I decided that I would also participate as part of a "marathon relay" team. Five of us would each run a section of the race. I signed up to run the first five or so miles. That way I could start with my dad, then go to the end of the course and encourage him during the final miles of his run. Good plan, right?

I was pretty fit at the time, so I didn't think much about training for a five mile jog. Piece of cake. No extra practice necessary.

This particular race was the Pittsburgh Marathon, scheduled to take place on May 5, 2013. As winter faded into spring, my dad shared with me that he was right on track with his training. Me? I pretty much sat on the couch and ate ice cream.

As the date grew closer, I came to realize that I would be leading a group of students on a trip to Haiti from April 29 to May 4, arriving back in Pittsburgh the night before the race. No big deal, I told myself. I'd be doing a lot of walking in Haiti, so that could kind of count as "prep work". Besides, it was five and half miles, was it even necessary to train?

I arrived back home late on the night of May 4th. I put my shorts, shoes, and t-shirt near the front door, along with a bottle of water and a nutrition bar. I wanted to be able to get ready quickly when my dad came to pick me up at 6 AM the next morning.

The sun was still rising to the east as we arrived at the starting area of the event on Sunday. My dad checked in with his yellow "full marathon" bib attached to his shirt, while my blue bib indicated that I would be running the first leg of the relay.

It was a warm, muggy, day. The sun was shining, which is a rare thing in Pittsburgh. My legs felt tired, and my shoes still had some Haitian dirt caked along the edges.

We started out with the rest of the thousands of runners. We moved at a fairly easy pace. My dad was indeed fit, but he was also 70. And he had to go all 26.2 miles. The course started on Pittsburgh's Northside, then up and over one of the city's many bridges. I chatted with my dad, but after a couple of miles, he asked me maybe if we could just focus on the running. I had three or so miles left, and he had 24, so he wanted to use his energy for running, not talking.

After 45 minutes, we arrived at the first relay area, where the next person on my team was waiting for me to start their portion of the run. It was then that I got a second wind, and decided to keep going, at least for a little while, to keep encouraging my dad.

As we approached mile seven or so, I came across a friend of mine, Julie, who was also running her first marathon.

"Hi!" I said, running alongside her.

"Hey," she replied. She looked uncomfortable. Struggling.

"Is everything OK?" I asked.

"Actually, not really. I have to go to the bathroom, but every time we pass a Port-a-John, there is a line, and I know if I stop too long, I will cramp up."

Hmm, I thought, an unfortunate problem.

I turned to my dad,
"You OK to take it from here? I am going to run up ahead and stand in line for Julie at a Port-a-John."

"That sounds like a good plan. I am fine."

I told him I would see him at the finish line. I told Julie I would run up ahead and wait in line at the next bathroom station, then when she got there she could take my place, hopefully avoiding a wait.

Off I went, running at a faster pace, weaving through the crowd of runners, passing person after person. It probably looked pretty obnoxious, like I was showing off that I was so much faster, when in reality it was because I knew that I only had to run to the closest Port-a-John.

About a half-mile later, I spotted one. There were seven or eight people waiting in line. I took my place at the end of the line and waited for Julie to arrive.

I waited, watching approaching runners closely to make sure that I didn't miss her.

I waited. And watched. And waited some more. No Julie.

Finally, I made it to the front of the line, but Julie was nowhere to be seen. I must have missed her. There were so many runners, and she could have easily passed without either of us seeing one another.

Well, at least I tried to help. Now what?

It occurred to me that the Pittsburgh Marathon course and Pittsburgh Half Marathon both shared the first nine miles, but the half marathon course then turned to cross a bridge, while the full marathon continued through the city to the same finish line.

At this point I was already about seven miles into the course. The shortest (and only) way to the finish line was to complete the half marathon. So that's what I decided to do.

Well rested from my break at the Port-a-John, I resumed my jogging along Pittsburgh's South Side, across the Birmingham

Bridge, and then turned to head back downtown to the finish line. Around mile nine my lungs started to burn and my legs began to ache. But I kept going. I thought of my dad, somewhere out there on the full marathon course, pushing through at age 70. I thought of the kids in Haiti that I had spent a week with, whose daily lives were a struggle for survival. I held in my mind my dad's face and the faces of those kids.

I thought of Isaiah 40:30-31:
He gives strength to the weary and increases the power of the weak. Even youths grow tired and weary, and young men stumble and fall; but those who hope in the Lord will renew their strength. They will soar on wings like eagles; they will run and not grow weary, they will walk and not be faint.

With each breath and each step, I truly relied upon a strength beyond my own to keep me going. I wouldn't say it was some kind of "magic" or "supernatural" intervention from God, but I would be bold enough to say that it wasn't just my body that was doing the running.

It was mysterious. But it was undeniably more than just me.

As I reached the final mile of the half marathon, I was running. Not jogging. Running. People alongside of the course gave me strange looks because I looked so unfazed, so full of energy.

I crossed the finish line. Without planning to, I completed a half marathon. Because of my blue-colored bib, I was directed to a table where they were handing out the relay medals. I picked one up, then looked around for the table where they were handing out the half marathon medals. I walked over and explained to a nice lady that I would really love to also have one of those, since I'd just also completed the 13.1 mile race. She seemed confused at first, but agreed and handed over the medal. I hung it around my neck, holding the relay medal in my hand.

But there was more to be done. I knew that in a little less than two hours my dad would be approaching the final stretch, so I walked back to right around mile 24.

As time went on, the crowd of racers thinned out substantially. Finally, almost two hours later, I looked up the street and saw my dad, slowly jogging towards me. His face showed the struggle.

I stepped out onto the street, "Hey dad!"

He looked at me with a look that said, "I've hit the wall."

"How much further?" he asked.

"You've got less than two miles, and it's all downhill," I encouraged, "I will run with you."

I jogged alongside him, reciting my best recollection of Isaiah 40:30-31. There were people lining the sides of the street, most of them looking for a runner they knew to give them a shout of encouragement.

"Hey y'all!", I shouted, "this is my dad! He's 70 and this is his first marathon! His name is George. Give him a cheer!"

At first, strange looks stared back at me, then I heard a man yell, "Go George!" And then another, "You got this, George!"

People clapped and cheered, and I could see that it gave him an extra dose of mental and physical energy.

Finally, the finish line was in sight. My dad picked up the pace, nearly sprinting, as we completed the final 100 yards. For him, 26.2 miles - for me, around 15 miles in total, not counting the two miles I walked back to run the final stretch with him.

We crossed the finish line and I gave him a big, sweaty hug. A volunteer, seeing my dad's yellow racing bib, placed a "marathon finisher" medal around his neck. We headed over to get Gatorade and fruit snacks in the recovery area.

When I got home that day, my wife was surprised to see two medals around my neck. I explained what happened, and she said, "Figures, you get home from Haiti one night, wake up, and accidentally run a half marathon."

The accidental half marathon.

I learned that day what the movie Finding Nemo taught a generation of kids (and adults) in the 1990s: just keep swimming. Or in this case, running.

What kept me going?

First, the desire to run alongside and encourage my dad.

Then, wanting to help Julie by holding her place in line at the bathroom.

Next, it was that the half marathon was my best (and only, really) option to get to the finish line.

Then, as I grew mentally and physically tired, it was the faces of those Haitian kids and the face of my dad.

Throughout, it was the mysterious power that I found in reciting the words of an ancient prophet.

And at times, it was the cheering from strangers.

And finally, at the end, it was the desire to run side by side with the person who'd run his race (of manhood, being a husband and father) so well over so many years.

That day taught me that running the race and getting to the end isn't about one thing, it's about many things that work together, sometimes in unexpected ways, to complete the journey.

Some would say, "focus on the goal" or "begin with the end in mind" or "when you encourage someone else, you become encouraged." On that day, I learned that all of these corny phrases are true in their own way. It's never just one thing. It's always a combination of motivations, inspirations, and practical principles that lead to finishing the race.

Whatever race you may be running, whether it's a literal race or a figurative one, gather all that you can as resources to get going, keep going, and finish.

sitting alone in the cafeteria

Most kids hate middle school. Not me. When I think back to middle school, I have many fond memories. Life was good. I had a good group of friends. I had good grades. I was good at skateboarding. I excelled in sports. I even had my first girlfriend.

Then, in the summer before 9th grade, my parents informed us that we were moving from Pittsburgh to West Springfield, Massachusetts. My dad had taken a new job. It all happened very suddenly, and I wasn't happy about it.

So in August of 1988 we packed up and headed to New England, leaving behind my charmed life in the Pittsburgh suburbs.

In Pittsburgh I had been attending a junior high, which at the time was grades 7, 8, and 9. So I had been anticipating that in 9th grade, I would finally be at the top of the pecking order. At Linton Junior High School, 9th graders ruled. I had been looking forward to that.

However, in Massachusetts, in the new district that I was set to attend, the high school was grades 9 through 12. So I was going from ruling the roost to "starting from the bottom."

I remember showing up on the first day of school. The kids in western Massachusetts looked different, dressed different, and acted different from the kids in Pittsburgh. If something was cool, it was "wicked." Pop was soda. The groups and cliques were much more defined than back in Pittsburgh. The jocks were only friends with the jocks. The nerds with the nerds, and so on.

Where I'd grown up, it wasn't like that. You could be a jock and a straight A student. You could be in the theater club and on the soccer team. I considered myself well-rounded. I was in the "honors" classes, played sports, rode my skateboard, listened to rap and alternative music, and had a diverse group of friends. At this new school, I wasn't sure where I would fit in.

My mom offered to give me a ride to school on the first day, but our house was within walking distance of the school, so I decided to ride my skateboard to school.

I arrived at the large building, and as I walked to my locker, a kid who looked like an 11th or 12th grader saw me carrying my board and snickered at me, "skater boy."

His friends laughed, and I kept walking.

As the day went on, it became obvious just how divided the groups were. Where would I find acceptance? I wasn't sure, and I was very nervous about it. As lunchtime approached, my anxiety level rose. Where would I sit in the cafeteria? Who would I sit with? I didn't know a single person.

Finally, my class before lunch ended. I went to my locker and retrieved my packed lunch. I figured that if I arrived at the cafeteria after most people were seated, I could just slide into a table and sit down with other 9th graders. Even that prospect seemed awkward, but what else could I do?

That was a mistake. By the time I got to the cafeteria, it was packed. Long rows of tables from one end to the other, with everyone sitting together in their cliques - jocks, nerds, preppies, theater kids.

I noticed at the far end of the room a lone circular table, where two kids were sitting.

Neither of them were talking to each other. One kid was drawing in a notebook and didn't even have a lunch.

I walked with trepidation from one end of the room to the other. I felt the eyes of people staring at me, like they knew for certain that I was the new kid. I finally reached the round table.

"Anyone sitting here?" I asked, motioning to one of the open spots. One kid looked up and shrugged his shoulders. I took that to indicate that the seat was available.

I sat down, opened my brown paper bag, and began to eat. The other kid looked up, "Are you new here?"

"Yeah," I said, "we just moved here from Pittsburgh."

"Cool, cool. I'm Matt," he said, looking me over. "You skate?"

"Um, yeah," I said.

He looked at the other kid at the table. "That's Eric. We skate."

Finally, I thought, maybe I wasn't going to be totally alone for all of 9th grade. Matt and I talked during lunch about what kind of skateboards we had, our favorite pro skaters, and the best skate spots around the area. Eric just sat there drawing in his notebook.

"Do either of you play basketball?" I asked. I was planning to play basketball that winter, and I hoped that one of them would give me some insight on how good the program was or what tryouts would be like.

They both laughed in unison, then Matt quipped, "Nah, man, basketball sucks."

His comment reinforced what I had been observing all day. This new school was super cliquey.

But at least, for today, I wasn't alone.

Lunch period ended, and I headed to my next class, feeling a sense of relief, at least for the afternoon.

When the school day ended, I started on my way home, riding my skateboard along the sidewalk. A bus, packed with students, passed by, and I heard a kid yell out from one of the windows, "Skater boy!" as he threw an empty soda bottle at me.

I stopped, stepped off of my board, and held my arms up, palms facing up, as if to say, "What was that for?"

Just then, my lunch table companions rode up behind me on their skateboards.

"Yeah, dude, it happens almost every day. You want to grab and go with us at Rosie's?"

"Sure," I said, not knowing what "grab and go" or "Rosie's" was. I followed them as we rode our skateboards. After a few blocks, we turned right, taking me a little bit off track from my route home. Just up ahead I saw a sign in front of a small convenience store:

"Rosie's"

We hopped off our boards a short distance away from the front door. That's when Matt filled me in on the plan.

"Mark, the lady that works here is totally ancient and super dumb. You go in first. Go right up to the counter and ask her about the cigarette selection. Be really loud and clueless. Eric and I will grab and go. Don't stop talking to her until we are out of the store."

Now I got it. "Grab and go" meant shoplift. Duh.

"Um," I said, hesitating.

"What, are you scared?" Matt challenged me.

"No, I just, um..."

"We'll grab stuff for you, don't worry." he reassured me.

I walked slowly towards the front door, opened it and stepped inside. There were three or four other customers, but none of them were at the check-out counter. I walked right up, seeing a short, elderly woman with a name tag on her red apron: "Rosie."

I did just as Matt instructed, while he and Eric snuck in quietly, swiftly shuffling along the aisles, grabbing bags of chips, candy, and bottled drinks and slipping them into their backpacks. They were in and out of the store in what seemed like a few seconds. Meanwhile, I asked Rosie a few ignorant sounding questions about the cigarette selection. Finally, I told her that they didn't have the kind I liked, and quickly left.

When I got outside, I saw Matt and Eric waiting for me about 100 feet up the street. I jumped on my skateboard and rode to them. They were already unloading a few snacks out of their backpacks. Matt tossed me a bottle of Mountain Dew and a Snickers bar.

"Great job, Mark. You've done this before!"

"Oh, yeah, thanks. It was easy," I replied, trying to sound like I had, "Uh, anyway, my house is back this way," motioning behind me.

"Cool, see ya," Matt said as he and Eric hopped onto their boards and headed off in the opposite direction, each sipping on a stolen bottle of soda as they rode.

I looked at the Mountain Dew in my left hand and the Snickers bar in my right hand. I felt guilty. My parents taught me better, I thought. What I did was wrong. But what now? I opened the Mountain Dew and took a swig. I shoved the Snickers in my backpack, and set off towards my house.

The next day, I got up and went to school, riding my skateboard once again. It was a warm, sunny late August day. I endured my classes, mainly ignored by the other students.

true stories

Matt and Eric weren't in any of my classes, and I didn't ever see them in the hallways between classes, but I figured I would see them again in the cafeteria. I was anticipating having at least a couple of people to sit with and talk to at lunch.

Lunch period arrived. Rather than wait like I did on the first day, I went straight to the round table at the end of the cafeteria, sitting down with my bagged lunch as other students started filing in.

Matt and Eric never showed up to lunch that day. It turns out they'd skipped school to take the bus to downtown Springfield to skate for the day. Of course, I had no idea about this, so there I was, sitting completely alone in a crowded cafeteria.

It's one thing to be alone, but that day I felt a visceral sense of loneliness that I had never experienced before. A packed cafeteria, with kids sitting and eating together, talking and laughing, with one student, me, all by myself at the one round table at the end of the room.

Several times I saw kids look over at me and then whisper to each other. I couldn't hear what they were saying, but I was sure it was something like, "Look at that kid, sitting by himself. What a loser."

I ate my lunch as quickly as I could, got up, and walked out of the large room, again having to pass by the long tables filled with my classmates.

I soon figured out that Matt and Eric weren't in 9th grade. They were in 11th grade, and they were barely ever in school. I didn't make the mistake of showing up to lunch early ever again.

I spent the rest of the school year eating my packed lunch while sitting on a bench in the school's lobby area. It was easier to be lonely alone than in a crowded cafeteria.

I also made sure that I left school each day after Matt and Eric, so that I wouldn't get pulled into their daily "grab and go" scheme. I'd tell them that my mom was giving me a ride home, or I would go a different way to avoid them seeing me.

I wish I could say that I ditched Matt and Eric, tried out for the basketball team, made a bunch of new friends, and things really turned around!

But that's not at all what happened. In fact, 9th grade was terrible. I didn't make any friends. I did play on the 9th grade basketball team, but my teammates were all already good friends with each other and didn't accept me.

I spent a lot of time alone. I spent a lot of time skateboarding by myself, or shooting baskets on the hoop that my dad nailed to a tree on the street outside our house.

The weeks turned into months, and I went from being an outgoing, well-liked 8th grader to a lonely, sad, angsty 9th grader.

Keenly aware of the dramatic shift in my mental health, my parents made the decision to move back to Pittsburgh after just 10 months in Massachusetts. Not only back to Pittsburgh, but back to the same community, which meant I'd be back in the same school district, back with my old friends. It was welcome news and a blessing.

Looking back so many years later, those months in Massachusetts seem like a bad dream. But they were also some of the most formative months of my life. Even though I didn't make an intentional, carefully considered decision to be alone rather than "fit in" with the wrong crowd, that is indeed what happened.

Matt and Eric were my only options for friends, as far as I could tell. And they were the wrong option. Some 30+ years later, I don't look back in judgment towards them. I have no idea what the circumstances of their lives were that led them to shoplift or frequently skip school. But I do know that if I had chosen to fit in with them rather than experience the pain of loneliness, it would have helped me in the short term, but cost me much more in the long term.

The apostle Paul, writing to a group of Jesus followers in Corinth, warns them with a phrase that I remember thinking about a lot during that 9th grade year:

"Bad company corrupts good character." 1 Corinthians 15:33

Paul is quoting a Greek poet, with whom his readers would be familiar. I love this because, not only is it true, but it is one of many places in the Christian scriptures where a writer uses the wisdom of the world to get a point across.

I knew, even as a 14-year-old, that my character was either going to grow or be corrupted, based on who I spent my time with. That's true even today, as a middle-age man. We become who we spend our time around.

Way back before Paul, the writer of the Hebrew scroll that we call Proverbs wrote an even longer section of wisdom, colorfully laying out just how bad it would be for a person to get caught up with the wrong crowd. Check out this translation from Eugene Peterson's The Message. As you read it, imagine the voice of an older, wiser person speaking to a younger person.

Proverbs 1, starting around verse 9...
Dear friend, if bad companions tempt you, don't go along with them. If they say,
"Let's go out and raise some hell. Let's beat up some old man, mug some old woman. Let's pick them clean and get them ready for their funerals. We'll load up on top-quality loot. We'll haul it home by the truckload. Join us for the time of your life! With us, it's share and share alike!"

Oh, friend, don't give them a second look; don't listen to them for a minute. They're racing to a very bad end, hurrying to ruin everything they lay hands on. Nobody robs a bank with everyone watching. Yet that's what these people are doing— they're doing themselves in. When you grab all you can get, that's what happens: the more you get, the less you are.

The writer paints a vivid picture of what it is like to get caught up with the wrong group of people, and it isn't pretty. It always ends badly. It happened to me on the first day of 9th grade. Thankfully, it didn't last longer.

Later on the writer says, **"He who walks with the wise grows wise, but a friend of fools suffers harm."** (Proverbs 20:13).

In every season or stage of life, carefully examine the people that you are surrounding yourself with, and be wise enough to choose loneliness over feeling acceptance into the wrong crowd. Be patient in your quest for companionship. Seek out others who will lift you up, not pull you down.

9th grade sucked. Being lonely sucked. But 9th grade taught me that it's OK to be lonely, and that it won't last forever.

Going through that season of isolation not only kept me from the destructive ways of the wrong people, but developed the character trait in me that I needed in other seasons of life.

In the decades since then, I have been blessed to find companions in the journey who lifted me up and brought wisdom into my life.

In college, I found a group of guys to meet with once a week for support and encouragement.

In my 20s, we joined a small group through our church where Kristin and I made lifelong friendships and could share in the common struggles and challenges of raising small children.

In my 30s, I sought professional counseling, a spiritual guide, and a mentor.

And now, in my 40s, I find connection through a weekly breakfast with a close friend and a consistent meeting with other pastors.

So, no matter what season of life you are in, you can and should endure loneliness, knowing that down the line you will be able to make the choice to involve yourself in circles of people that guide you towards the kind of person you want to become.

true stories

tap tap

The first time that I traveled outside of the United States, I was 25 years old. I co-led a youth group mission trip to Juarez, Mexico. I loved every minute of it, especially the opportunity to experience a new culture in a raw and real way. We stayed in a building in the middle of a neighborhood. We ate authentic, home-cooked meals. We walked the streets and interacted with locals.

It awakened in me not just a love for travel and new experiences, but the desire to see new places up close. The richness of that time in Mexico was all about being immersed in the culture, at least as much as is possible, for a week.

I led excursions to Mexico each of the next three summers, once on a return trip to Juarez, and twice even further south to the coastal city of Tepic. Each trip was amazing in its own way, but the common thread was the up-close nature of the experience. By the fourth adventure, I started to consider myself a "travel to Mexico" pro. And one of the best parts was that I was the leader, so I got to arrange almost every aspect of the itinerary, from how we got there to where we stayed, as well as all of our activities.

In the summer of 2006 I had the chance to participate in a trip to Haiti, assisting in taking a group of just-graduated high school guys and their dads.

If Mexico was dipping my toe in the water of a new culture, Haiti would definitely be going in deeper.

As we prepared for the trip, it started to dawn on me that there would be many elements I'd never been exposed to before:

- A new language, Creole, of which I knew exactly zero.

- Being in the vast minority, as a caucasian.

- A breadth of poverty unlike anything that I'd ever seen before.

To top it off, we'd be flying from Florida to Cap Haitian, our destination city, in a DC3 aircraft: a non-pressurized World War II relic.

But I was ready for this new adventure. I was also confident in tackling the unknown because our leader, my friend Jayson, had been to the exact place where we were going several times. He was the "pro" as far as traveling to Haiti, and I placed my trust in his expertise.

The day of departure arrived. Our group was fifteen people: nine recent high school graduates, four of their dads, Jayson and me. We met at the airport in Pittsburgh, then flew on a typical commuter jet to Miami, arriving in the evening.

After a restful night at a Hampton Inn, we woke up before the sun and took a shuttle van to a small airport in Fort Pierce, about two hours north of Miami.

We walked through a big hangar and out onto the tarmac, loading our own bags onto the plane. It had a metal floor and no door between the cabin and cockpit. Our pilot introduced himself to us and explained that we would have to make a stop in Exuma in the Bahamas to refuel. My anxiousness kicked up a notch. The plane didn't hold enough fuel for a 700 mile flight?

After boarding the aircraft, Jayson explained that the best idea would be for him to collect our passports and keep them all in his backpack, so that when we arrived in Haiti they could be securely locked away in a safe at the place where we were staying. He said that kidnappings of foreigners, while rare, did happen and that one of the most sought after items was a US passport.

The co-pilot counted us and realized that the plane was one seat short. He went back into the hangar and emerged with another airplane seat, carried it onboard, and bolted it to the floor.

This did not help in calming my already anxious heart.

Once we were all settled in our seats, we taxied to the end of the runway. The plane's propellers spun loudly, and we charged across the pavement. The aircraft slowly lifted off the ground, tilting slightly back as it ascended.

And it stayed that way. The plane leaned back at about a ten degree angle, like a skateboard tilted up in its rear wheels. Jayson, having flown in this exact plane previously, turned to me and yelled to me through the buzzing air of the unpressurized cabin, "This is totally normal! It's just how it was designed to fly!"

As we cruised above the Atlantic Ocean, it dawned on me that this trip was already teaching me about trust and letting go of control. On the previous trips that I'd made outside of the United States, I was out of my comfort zone, but I was the one planning and leading. *I* booked the flights. *I* arranged the itinerary. I even decided who was sitting where on the airplane. Now, I was being forced to let go and trust others who had already been where I was now going. It turns out that plane ride was just a preview.

After our refueling stop in Exuma, we climbed once again above the ocean, the whole time at a cruising altitude where we could still see the crystal blue water below us, dotted with yachts and large sailing vessels. A sharp contrast to what we were about to see as we landed in Cap Haitian.

Soon the coastline of northern Haiti appeared. Rugged, deforested mountains and valleys of farmland came into view through the small airplane windows.

We approached the landing strip, and as we got closer I saw a man walking his cow through the grass *inside* the airport landing area. Then, even closer to where we were about to touch down, I spotted a group of children playing soccer in the dirt right next to the landing strip.

That was just the beginning. We landed, rear wheels first, then the nose of the plane. We came to a stop and the doors opened. Humid heat poured into the cabin.

Stepping off of the plane and onto Haitian soil, the sensory overload was absolutely overwhelming. New sounds, sites, and smells every second. Jayson assured me that our contact person would be there, waiting to take us and our luggage to the place where we'd be staying for the week.

The airport itself was just a small one-story building, about the size of a fast food restaurant, but one that hadn't been remodeled since the 1950s.

Inside the small airport it was madness. Dozens of men were talking loudly to each other, checking our baggage, inspecting our backpacks, and all hoping to earn some money from the visiting Americans.

Finally, a Haitian man saw Jayson and they greeted each other with a hug. His name was Daniel, and he spoke English. He explained to Jayson that the truck was waiting outside. He told us to wear our backpacks on the front of our bodies and to not let anyone who offered help to touch or carry any of our belongings. If we did, they would be expecting a big cash tip.

He ushered us through the crowded exit to the street, where a large flatbed truck with a chest-high metal frame built into the bed waited for us. We loaded our bags, taking the entire space inside the metal framing.

I turned to Jayson,

"They are taking the luggage in the truck, but what about us? Is there a bus or a couple of vans?"

Jayson smiled.

"Nope" he said, as he climbed into the back of the truck, "We are riding back here with our stuff."

The situation appeared to be two things: unsafe and a tight squeeze.

I waited as our group of high school grads climbed into the bed of the truck. Soon it was clear that there wouldn't be enough room for all of us. Ken, one of the dads, and I were left standing next to the truck with Daniel, our Haitian host.

"No problem," he said, "follow me."

Ken and I left our group and followed Daniel along the busy sidewalk next to the airport. He led us to a small red pick up truck, with benches lining the sides of the bed in the back. There was a man in the driver's seat.

Daniel turned to us, "This is Rueben's tap tap. You can ride in here. He will follow the truck."

Ken and I looked at each other, both thinking "What's a tap-tap?" then climbed into the back, sitting across from each other on the benches.

Daniel walked to the driver's side door and said something to Reuben in Creole. He then headed back towards the rest of our group, leaving us with a reassuring smile and a thumbs up.

The big truck pulled out with the rest of our group standing inside the framing, looking down at Ken and me as we sat in the back of the pickup.

Reuben pulled behind them and began to follow. As we left the airport area and turned onto the busy streets of the city, I was again overwhelmed with sights and sounds and smells. It was the middle of the day, and people were everywhere. The traffic was chaotic. Cars and trucks and small motorcycles buzzed past each other, with no lanes or rules or patterns. The streets were partially paved, but giant potholes and large patches of dirt dotted the path as we swerved in and around masses of people and animals and other vehicles.

I looked over at Ken, and that's when my worry grew. The look on his face wasn't one of adventure or excitement. He looked straight up scared.

"Mark, do you realize that we are in Haiti, sitting in the back of this truck driven by a stranger? We don't know where he is taking us, our phones don't work, and our passports are in Jayson's bag."

He was right. And as Reuben navigated through the traffic, I noticed that the truck that was carrying the rest of our group was getting farther and farther away, sometimes even getting out of sight.

Ken and I were indeed thousands of miles from home, without identification, sitting in the back of a truck (without seatbelts, of course), with a stranger driving us.

At that moment, traffic slowed down as we approached a major intersection. There was no traffic signal, just vehicles from four directions all attempting to get where they wanted, vying for position and nudging past each other like rugby players in a scrum.

The next thing I knew, a Haitian man walked up to the back corner of our truck, tapped on the side of it, and attempted to get in! Ken and I were being attacked! Ken kicked him and the traffic started to pick up, and Reuben was able to speed away.

The guy yelled something in Creole, clearly irate at us for fighting him off. All I could think about was Jayson telling me that while kidnappings of foreigners were rare, they did happen.

We'd been in the country for less than 15 minutes and already I was thinking that maybe this trip was a bad idea.

At the next intersection, it happened again.

This time it was a lady holding a baby! We were stopped waiting for traffic ahead to get moving, she tapped on the tailgate of the truck and attempted to climb on, with her baby!

Ken, rather than kicking her as he did our first would-be kidnapper, just yelled, "No! No! Get away!" and motioned with his hand to let her know that he meant business.

She yelled something back in Creole and stepped away, a confused look on her face.

Finally, we arrived at our destination, an orphanage on the outskirts of the city. The big truck was already there and the rest of our group had climbed down and were now surrounded by a throng of smiling, loud Haitian children. Meanwhile, Ken and I felt lucky to be alive, having survived two near-kidnappings!

Reuben, our driver, got out of his truck and went straight to Daniel. They spoke in Creole and then both broke out into a fit of laughter.

As Ken and I got out of the truck, Daniel and Reuben approached us with wide grins.

"Friends, I should have told you! Reuben is a tap-tap driver. A tap-tap is like a taxi in the U.S. His truck is a taxi. Those people who were trying to climb onto the truck were his customers!"

We explained to the rest of our group what had happened and everyone had a good laugh at our expense. Daniel and Reuben spoke to each other again in Creole, and then Daniel said that Reuben wanted to let us know that we owed him money for losing his potential customers. We felt terrible.

"Just kidding!" Reuben said. He and Daniel cracked up again.

We unloaded our luggage and carried it to where we'd be staying for the week. The rest of the trip was an amazing experience, and over the next 20 years I have returned to Haiti more than 10 times and taken more than 150 college students there to learn and grow and experience the amazing culture and people.

But on that first trip, I wasn't the leader. I was the participant, and I had to place trust into the hands of other people who knew more than I did. I had to lean on their experience and expertise.

Many times in life that is the case. Our ability to step outside of our comfort zone has to include trust of people who have already been to the place where we hope to go. The right guide, the expert pilot, the leader who has already walked the road that we are daring to venture down. And they might not be the person that we expect.

It makes me think of Paul in the New Testament of the Bible. On the journey that changed his life forever, he was headed to a city called Damascus to do what he thought was "righteous" work, doing his best to suppress a new sect of Jesus followers. When God crashed into his life, Paul not only had a complete paradigm shift of who God was and who Jesus was, but he also had to trust a process that included the involvement of strangers God had placed in his path as part of his transformation.

Paul, who at the time was named Saul, has a supernatural encounter with Jesus. He is blinded, then led into Damascus, the city where he originally planned to go to round up Jesus' followers to take them to jail. For three days he is blind. He doesn't eat or drink anything. Imagine how he is processing these events. I bet that he was thinking that the same people he came to capture were now going to be his captors! Jesus' words to him weren't clear when he met him. He says to Saul,

"Now get up and go into the city, and you will be told what you must do." - Acts 9:6

Maybe Saul is thinking that Jesus is about to exact revenge or retribution upon Saul for the way that he has already persecuted Jesus' followers. "You will be told what you must do" sounds kind of ominous. In his old way of thinking, when Jesus speaks this to him, it might have seemed like a warning of consequences for what he's been doing. Like, "You will be told what punishment is in store for you." After all, Saul is blinded, which seems like it might be step one in God's revenge against him for what he'd been doing.

Then, he is led to the city where a man named Ananias, part of the Jesus followers group, is told that he is going to be Saul's host and caretaker.

From both men's perspective, they had to trust what God was saying to them, and then take the action step of trusting each other throughout the process. Ananias was scared that Saul would harm him. He says to God, in Acts, chapter 9, verses 13 and 14:

"Lord, I have heard many reports about this man and all the harm he has done to your holy people in Jerusalem. And he has come here with authority from the chief priests to arrest all who call on your name."

God reassures him that Saul, who He will eventually renamed Paul, will be his chosen instrument to proclaim the message of Jesus all around the world. Once Paul's vision was restored, he went on to live life with a new purpose. Instead of persecuting Christians, he spent the remainder of his life sharing the good news of Jesus with everyone that he met.

Paul was wary of Ananias and Ananias was wary of Paul. But God brought them together in this way to totally flip the script on what role they would play in the story.

Like Ken and me in the back of that tap-tap. We thought that we were surrounded by threats, but the opposite was true. Reuben wasn't out to get us, he was there to keep us safe and get us to our destination. Daniel had placed us into the hands of a trusted guide, not a kidnapper.

In your life, are there people who you perceive as threats? While it is true that not everyone is safe or good for us, maybe God could be placing them in your life as instruments of aid? Do you automatically assume that people are "up to no good?"

Maybe we need to change our thinking. Maybe we need to realize that some people have been placed in our path not as threats, but as guides and even "vehicles" of transformation, for our benefit.

If you default to going it alone or live with a self-preservation mindset, perhaps it might be wise to open up to the possibility that some people have been placed in our lives for a greater purpose.

Each time I slip into thinking that the world is against me, I remember that tap-tap ride in Haiti.

Trust that He has placed people in your path as the means by which He is guiding you to the next steps on your journey.

dunked

I grew up playing sports.

I wasn't the biggest, fastest, or strongest kid.

But I was skilled, coordinated, and naturally athletic.

Just about everything came easily to me. In the fall it was soccer, in the winter basketball, and in the spring baseball. I wasn't ever the best, but I was usually good enough to make the "travel" or "all-star" team.

Then puberty hit. Then for literally what seemed like everyone but me. I went from being a thin, slightly-below-average-sized kid to a late bloomer. When I started 9th grade, I was barely five feet tall. A growth spurt during that year pushed me up to 5'9", but that turned my already thin into extremely skinny. I just didn't fill out. I had no desire to workout, and wasn't ever a big eater.

Soon enough, my slight frame and lack of time in the weight room caught up to me. I quit soccer in 9th grade and basketball and baseball soon followed.

I was still athletic, but I was far from an athlete. In 10th grade, they had a spot for me on the JV volleyball team, so I opted for the one team sport where the opposing team had to stay over on their side of the court.

I graduated high school at a whopping 120 pounds, and headed off to college as a NARP (non-athlete regular person).

While there I finally started to fill out a little, and spent hours playing pickup and intramural basketball. I still had my natural ability, and volleyball had helped me develop into a pretty good jumper. Still just 5'9", I could easily jump up and grab the rim of a regulation 10-foot basketball hoop, and if my adrenaline was pumping, could even manage to dunk a volleyball. Humble brag.

Sports became fun again. I came into my own, especially on the basketball court, and sometimes wondered why I quit playing in the first place.

Following my sophomore year of college, I decided to spend a month of my summer volunteering at a Young Life summer camp in North Carolina. Nestled away in the Smoky Mountains, Windy Gap was an idyllic setting and I had an amazing volunteer "job": ropes course wrangler.

Each morning and afternoon the college "Summer Staff" would lead activities for high school campers, including horseback riding, go-karts, and of course, a high ropes course, which was the team I was on.

Once my afternoon assignment was finished, I usually had a couple of hours of free time before dinner, so I would head over to the basketball court.

There were two great things about playing basketball that month during my free time:

true stories

1. I was playing with and against high school kids, so it was almost certain that I was always one of the best, if not the best, players on the court.

2. The court had adjustable hoops that went as low at 8 feet, so dunking the ball was easy.

After three weeks of this daily routine, my basketball skills were peaking. I was 20 years old and finally reaching my athletic potential.

But of course that's not why I was at Windy Gap. I was there to serve kids and help them learn more about how much God loves them. I was there as a college student to be an example to high school kids of what a college-age follower of Jesus was supposed to be like.

There was one particular afternoon when these two things didn't exactly line up the way that they should have.

I had just finished my afternoon of facilitating a group on the ropes course and headed down to the basketball court.

There were a few kids shooting baskets. They looked like they had wandered onto the basketball court out of boredom. I suggested that we play a game of full-court 4-on-4 on the 8-foot rims. They reluctantly agreed. The dunk show was about to commence.

I don't remember all of the details of that game, but something happened that I won't ever forget. I mean, something didn't just "happen" - it's probably better stated that I did something that I won't ever forget.

true stories

Partway into the game I gathered a defensive rebound and went coast to coast. A kid on the other team, about the same size that I was when I started 9th grade, tried to defend me on my way to the hoop. I hesitated, created a bit of space, let him back off, and then dribbled hard, driving to the hoop, soaring through the air and dunking the ball, two-handed, right on his head.

Not satisfied with this feat of Michael Jordanesque proportions, I acted as if I was turning to run back on defense. The kid I had just dunked on took the ball and lazily passed it in from under his hoop. I saw this soft pass out of the corner of my eye and intercepted it on its way to its intended recipient. He stepped out from under the hoop, realizing his mistake just in time to try to defend me from another dunk.

He failed, and I once again flushed the ball through the hoop as he stood helplessly below me. Two dunks right on his head in a matter of seconds.

At that moment it was as if time froze. He looked at me, then looked right at my chest, shaking his head as his eyes read the words in large block letters on the front of my t-shirt: SUMMER STAFF. I was still wearing my royal blue staff t-shirt, clearly identifying me as such.

My pride turned to utter embarrassment. What an idiotic, bone-headed, mean thing I'd just done. This victimized kid was just trying to waste some time and shoot hoops with his friends, and now this person (me) who was supposed to be the cool college-age example of a "Christian" had just humiliated him. Twice.

I knew what I had done, but I didn't have the courage to do anything about it, at least not at that moment.

It was clear that my outside appearance didn't match what I claimed to be on the inside. I let my ego and my insecurity take over, and the result was a moment of stupidity and regret.

I was, in that moment, the definition of a hypocrite.

It's not a good feeling to realize that's what you are. Especially in light of Jesus' strong warnings about people like this. Jesus lived in a time when there were a whole group of people that "wore" their religion on their sleeves (quite literally), but whose hearts were twisted and unchanged.

Matthew's Gospel records a speech that Jesus gave in reaction to the way that these people claimed to be better than others but whose insides were corrupt. In this stinging message, found in the 23rd chapter, he calls out the religious fakers in front of the crowds. Take a look at it for yourself. Jesus doesn't pull any punches. His words are strong and he turns to directly address these "religious" leaders with this summary:

Matthew 23:25-28
"You clean the outside of the cup and dish, but inside they are full of greed and self-indulgence. Blind Pharisee! First clean the inside of the cup and dish, and then the outside also will be clean.

You are like whitewashed tombs, which look beautiful on the outside but on the inside are full of the bones of the dead and everything unclean. In the same way, on the outside you appear to people as righteous but on the inside you are full of hypocrisy and wickedness."

This is Jesus bringing the heat. He's in their faces, and we can read these words a couple of thousand years later and shake our heads, "Yeah, those Pharisees sure were a rotten bunch!"

But like an old mentor of mine used to say, we have to be careful when we point our finger because there are three fingers pointing back at us.

That bone-headed moment on the basketball court wasn't the only time in my life I have acted like a total hypocrite. In all honesty, I have had so many similar missteps that I can't even keep them all straight!

In the case of the "Basketball Incident of 1994", God allowed me to see my mistake and take action to change my attitude. It's not something that has happened every time that I've done such an idiotic thing, but in that case, there's a little more to the story.

Later that evening, I found that kid while everyone was waiting outside of the dining hall for the evening meal. As I approached him and made eye contact, I could tell he was still feeling the sense of humiliation from my earlier actions.

I walked up to him and placed my hand on his shoulder, then actually got super nervous. I asked him if I could talk to him away from his friends for a minute. He reluctantly agreed.

"Hey man, what's your name?"

"Mark," he said.

"Really?" I replied, "That's my name, too. I just wanted to apologize for earlier. I was a real jerk on the basketball court."

"It's OK," he shrugged.

"Actually, it's not OK. I'm really sorry. Please forgive me and know that is not the example that I want to be."

"I mean, it's really OK, but thanks, that means a lot."

He walked back to his friends.

I wish I could say that I later learned that the *Mark* that I dunked on went on to become some amazing leader and credited his life turnaround on the quick-to-apologize example that I showed him, but in reality I have no idea what happened to him. I don't think that I ever saw him at Young Life camp again.

Whether or not anything changed in his life as the result of that apology or not, it was a big moment of growth for me.

The Young Life camp where I was on Summer Staff was very intentional with everything that happened at camp each week: the purpose was to show and tell high school students that the God of the universe loved them and that Jesus was the full expression of that love.

In some small, flawed way, I had modeled what it's like to be a person who is able to admit that they need forgiveness. I truly believe that God redeemed my moment of jerk-ness with a moment of sincere human remorse and connection.

The Apostle Paul had a lot to say about forgiveness in the letters that he wrote. As someone with a pretty radical testimony of how God had rescued him and offered him forgiveness and a fresh start, he knew what it was like to be on both ends of the pain that humans can cause each other.

This sentence from Ephesians 4 stands out to me and has stuck with me over the years:

Be kind to one another, tenderhearted, forgiving one another, as God in Christ forgave you. - Ephesians 4:32

Kindness and a person who is described as tenderhearted? Someone known to forgive? How do we get there?

By remembering "as God in Christ forgave you."

All of us mess up. Big and small ways, day in and day out. The good news is that we are forgiven because of Jesus. Because of that forgiveness, we get to experience and extend forgiveness in human relationships.

The old saying goes that "Christianity is more caught than taught." In the area of forgiveness, this is absolutely true.

May all of us learn to have the courage and humility to say "I'm sorry" and the grace to forgive when we've been wronged, even as we have been forgiven.

cai jorge debravo

"Tenemos una oportunidad para que usted y el equipo sirvan a los prisioneros mientras estén aquí en Costa Rica. Sabemos que tiene algunos jóvenes con usted que disfrutan del fútbol, y hemos organizado una visita a una prisión local para un juego entre su grupo y algunos de los reclusos".

I was sitting in a meeting with the ministry director of a church in the central part of Costa Rica where I had taken a group of high school students on a trip in the summer of 2008. Even with my limited knowledge of Spanish, several of the words stood out to me. I heard something about "opportunities" and "futbol" and "prison."

I gathered that perhaps there would be an opportunity to visit a prison to play soccer with some of the inmates. I was hoping that my Spanish was off, and that the words "prisioneros" and "prisión" meant something different. After hearing the translation from our interpreter, I realized that I had heard correctly:

"We have an opportunity for you and the team to serve prisoners while you are here in Costa Rica. We know that you have some young people with you who enjoy soccer, and we have arranged a visit to a local prison for a game between your group and some of the inmates."

My previous experience serving in other countries included painting a church, doing crafts with children, and building a retaining wall. Here in Costa Rica, it was about to get real.

Our group included both guys and girls, but since this was a male-only prison, just the men from our group would be going to the jail for the soccer game.

Mike, the co-leader of our group, and I were adults. The rest of our guys were between the ages of 14 and 18. We were heading to a real prison, where we were told almost every man there was serving at least 10 years for crimes like armed robbery, drug trafficking, and even homicide.

I had never been inside the walls of a jail. I pictured the facility in Costa Rica like something I might have seen in the movies. A dark, dungeon-like structure with 40-foot high walls, a watchtower with a rifle-equipped guard, and tattooed gang members ready to fight anyone who looked at them the wrong way.

As we loaded into the van that day, I hoped that my anxiousness was not obvious to the group of teenagers that I was leading. We drove through the streets of the city of Cartago, then down a country road. After about 10 minutes we arrived at CAI Jorge Debravo. I had learned from our host that this prison was part of the CAI, Consejo de Atención Integral. In English, this roughly translates as Comprehensive Care Center. And that Jorge Debravo was a famous Costa Rican poet that was from this area. A prison named after a poet. Weird.

Upon arrival, we entered through the gate to find a series of one and two-story buildings surrounded by a tall wall, with barbed-wire across the top. But it was much more of a country campus vibe than what I had imagined from scenes in The Shawshank Redemption.

We parked and checked in at the entrance, each of us getting the typical pat-down from the security guard. We were escorted to a conference room in the administrative building, where the staff explained to us the history of this prison, the philosophy of rehabilitation that Costa Rica had been implementing, and the details about our soccer match.

They let us know that, indeed, the men in the prison were all serving hard time for serious crimes. This facility was for those kinds of crimes and jail sentences only. We would be playing our soccer match in a gymnasium. The game would be five versus five with a goalie. Those who weren't playing would be sitting in the bleachers and have a chance to talk with those inmates who were there to watch.

We were then led to the gym. The team of inmates was already out on the floor, passing a soccer ball to each other in a circle. Some wore soccer jerseys, while others were shirtless. Another twenty or so men were sitting in the bleachers.

As we entered through the door, the supervisor, who I would later learn was named Gabriel, blew a whistle, and immediately they stopped their activity and gave their full attention. He instructed them, in Spanish, to sit along the front row of the bleachers.

Through an interpreter, he asked us to stand facing them, shoulder to shoulder. We complied.

Looking back, I have to admit that I was nervous about what might happen next. I feared that our young men, teenagers and mostly still in high school, were going to be playing soccer against violent, hardened criminals. As I looked at our guys, I could see the fear in their faces, too.

Gabriel then turned to us and asked us to introduce ourselves, one by one. Starting with Mike, my co-leader, we went down the line and each person said their name and where they were from. A couple of our guys even spoke in Spanish, bringing a smile to the faces of several of the prisoners.

We concluded our introductions, and one of the men raised his hand to ask a question. I anticipated something like, "Have any of you ever been in a prison before?" or "Are you scared of us?" But instead, in English, he asked: "Which of you is the best soccer player?"

That broke the ice, and the whole mood of the room shifted. I looked at our team, then at one of our 18-year-olds who had played soccer throughout high school.

"I would go with Jake," I answered, then pausing to attempt to relay the same information in Spanish, "Creo que es Jake"

"Which one is Jake?" the same man replied.

Raising his hand hesitantly, Jake acknowledged. But at the same moment, Matt, another student on our team who was more fluent in Spanish, said, "Jake es un buen atleta, pero yo soy más hábil en el fútbol."

The whole group of inmates cracked up. Those of us less fluent in Spanish turned to Matt, signaling to him to tell us what he said.

"I just told the truth. I said that Jake is a good athlete, but I am a more skilled soccer player."

He turned back to the guys on the bleachers, "Solo digo la verdad." (I am only telling the truth)

They laughed again.

Gabriel then directed us to the other side of the gym, telling us that we had a couple of minutes to warm up and decide on our first five starting players and goalie.

The inmates who were a part of their team also returned to the gym floor, while the others stayed on the bleachers to watch.

We had 12 guys, including Mike and myself, so we decided on a first string and second string. Mike started as the goalie and I would serve as the back up goalie in case he got tired. That suited me just fine, as it matched quite well with my level of soccer skill.

A few minutes later, Gabriel blew his whistle again, and the starting lineups came to the center of the gym. He placed the ball on the floor for our team to open the game with a typical soccer kickoff.

The game was fast paced and very evenly matched. The inmates had experience and a higher level of skill, but most of our boys were helped by their youthful energy and superior speed. The most amazing thing about the game was that the inmates did as much laughing, smiling, and congratulating each other and our team as they did actually playing soccer.

I was anticipating competitive intensity, but instead the overall vibe in the gym was that of fun and fellowship.

I specifically remember an incident when one of our guys was fouled close to their goal and tumbled to the ground. The offending player not only helped him up to his feet, but gave him a hug as he helped him line up for a penalty kick.

As I watched, Gabriel came over to me, sitting with me in the bleachers. Our interpreter wasn't around, but he seemed to have something important to say to me, so I initiated, "Hablo español un poco, y yo comprendo un poco."

"I speak a little bit of Spanish, and I understand a little."

From my limited knowledge of Spanish, I thought that he was trying to explain to me that as soon as the game was over, there would be a time of sharing. I gathered that the inmates would sit on the bleachers and then one of our players would get a chance to share their story.

At halftime, I asked our guys if there was anyone who would be willing to step up and share with the group after the game. One of our youngest team members, Zack, said he would share.

The second half was just as evenly played as the first half. I did get a turn to play goalie, which didn't go as badly as I thought it would.

When the game ended, I asked one of our guys if we won. "I don't think anyone was keeping score," he replied. That seemed about right. This game wasn't about winning or losing; it was about coming together and enjoying the game and the fellowship.

Gabriel once more blew his whistle and instructed everyone to be seated on the bleachers. By this time, our group and the inmates had established a good rapport, and I remember looking at them as they sat intermingled in the stands. It was a picture of diversity and unity, and it was beautiful.

Our interpreter reappeared, standing next to Gabriel. He projected his voice and addressed the crowd:

"Gracias a nuestros huéspedes estadounidenses por visitarnos. Nos alegra que haya podido jugar fútbol con nosotros hoy. Nos dio un buen calentamiento para nuestro próximo partido en la liga que jugamos con otros centros de atención integral."

The interpreter relayed his message:
"Thank you to our American guests for visiting us. We are glad that you were able to play soccer with us today. It gave us a good warm up for the upcoming game in our league with other comprehensive care centers."

Gabriel continued, "Y ahora nos complace saber de Mateo, uno de nuestros hombres, quien compartirá con nosotros su historia."

"And now we are pleased to hear from Mateo, one of our men, who will be sharing with us his story."

It was then that I realized that my interpretation of my conversation with Gabriel at halftime was a bit off. It turned out that he wasn't telling me that one of our players would share, but instead that one of the inmates would.

Mateo, who looked to be in his late 20s, stepped forward. He was still sweating from the soccer game, with a small towel draped around his neck. He seemed nervous. The interpreter stood next to him as he shared his story.

I don't remember what he said word for word. But I do recall most of it. I write here in English my best recollection of what Mateo shared that day in a prison gymnasium in the mountains of Costa Rica:

"My name is Mateo, but most people in my life have just called me Tres, because I am the youngest of three brothers. My life has not been easy. When I was a little boy, everyone around me was getting in trouble. My mom and dad had a hard time finding good jobs, and we were very poor. My older brothers did not set a good example, and soon I found myself in the streets, getting into trouble as well. At first, it was little things, but as I got older, my problems got bigger.

When I was a teenager, I got in with the wrong people, and participated in a lifestyle of drugs and theft. I got caught and sent away. But as soon as I was able to get out, I was back to the streets and the same bad choices.

Finally, the life that I was living caught up with me. I robbed a man in his car, and the police found me. I was out of chances, and I was sentenced to six years, here in this place. I have been here for three years so far.

At first, when I came here, I was angry. But soon I started attending the chapel that Gabriel does each week.

That is where I learned who I really am. I am a child of God, and a son of the King. Like Paul said in the Bible, 'I am the boss of all of the sinners, but I am saved by God's grace through Jesus.'

Now, even though I still have time left in this place, I am experiencing freedom in my spirit, because I know my identity.

My friends from America, you can have this same freedom. All you have to do is accept that you are loved, and then live a new life.

I want to end with this verse from Galatians, chapter 3, verses 28 and 29:

In Christ's family there can be no division into Jew and non-Jew, slave and free, male and female. Among us you are all equal. That is, we are all in a common relationship with Jesus Christ.

Thank you for listening, and please take a moment to think about what I said."

Mateo returned to his seat, and as he did, the whole group gave him a rousing round of applause.

Gabriel concluded our time with a prayer, and let us know that the inmates would be leaving soon to get cleaned up for the rest of the day. He joked that unfortunately, we would not be able to shower there and would have to drive back in the van all sweaty and stinky.

The inmates and our students climbed down from the bleachers, and I stood off to the side with Gabriel as we watched our guys and the inmates exchange hugs. Less than two hours earlier, we'd entered the facility with trepidation, and now we were leaving with a completely different paradigm of these men and this place.

That day was a clear picture to me of what it looks like when people exist together under the banner of God's love and grace. Yes, it was just for a couple of hours, but it was a tangible experience of a unity that is based on more than just common humanity, but also common grace.

Throughout this book, I have included verses and passages from the Bible to undergird the lessons that I have learned through different experiences. I have tried to keep those brief, for the most part. Here, I want to include a longer passage that captures the essence of the kind of unity that I am talking about.

It comes from a letter that Paul wrote to the church in Ephesus. From what we can gather, Paul spent about ten years of his life starting, investing in, and then writing to this church community. It wasn't a community that was perfect by any means, but it was a vibrant church in a multiethnic city. Listen to what Paul says to the church in his letter:

Ephesians 2:14-22
For He (Jesus) himself is our peace, who has made the two groups one and has destroyed the barrier, the dividing wall of hostility, by setting aside in his flesh the law with its commands and regulations. His purpose was to create in himself one new humanity out of the two, thus making peace, and in one body to reconcile both of them to God through the cross, by which he put to death their hostility. He came and preached peace to you who were far away and peace to those who were near. For through him we both have access to the Father by one Spirit.

Consequently, you are no longer foreigners and strangers, but fellow citizens with God's people and also members of his household, built on the foundation of the apostles and

prophets, with Christ Jesus himself as the chief cornerstone. In him the whole building is joined together and rises to become a holy temple in the Lord. And in him you too are being built together to become a dwelling in which God lives by his Spirit.

What a beautiful description of what is possible through the love that God brings to humanity through Jesus.

That is something that I want to be a part of! Don't you?

The power of grace to bring people together was true in the church in Ephesus in the first century. It was true in a gymnasium in a prison in Costa Rica in the summer of 2008, and it is true today, wherever people come together under the unifying banner of grace.

And it is true right now, wherever you are. Take a step to boldly engage in community, moving out of the false comfort of isolation, and into the possibility of a shared life in the diverse and beautiful family of God.

true stories

kona

As I was preparing to graduate from college in 1996, the next logical step for me was to go into full-time youth ministry. I know, it seems crazy to most people. But it was a clear sense that I had at the time. I had so many positive experiences as a teenager through my involvement in church youth groups. I had fun. I made good friends. I met cute girls. I genuinely learned about God. So why not just keep it going, but as a job?

I also knew that I wanted to learn from someone who had been working with young people for a while. There was a church in the Pittsburgh area with a reputation for a vibrant ministry led by a youth pastor with a proven track record of "success": Patrick Dominguez. I learned from my brother Steve that the church where Patrick worked, St. Stephen's, was offering a full-time one-year internship for college grads. It was a perfect opportunity. I completed my application.

An added incentive was that the girl I was dating, Kristin, happened to be from the small town where St. Stephen's was located.

It worked out just as I had hoped: I was chosen for the internship, and she got a job as the Head Women's Soccer Coach at Geneva College. Nine months later, the church hired me to be the new Middle School Youth Pastor.

It was a great fit. I had many gifts and talents that made me a good youth pastor: extroverted, able to speak to kids, somewhat goofy (immature?), and passionate about meeting people where they were as they explored who God was.

Kristin and I got married in 1997. We rented an apartment right across the street from the church.

I involved myself in the local community, coaching middle school lacrosse, middle school basketball, and middle school girls soccer. I became known as a "good guy," someone who cared about teenagers and was counted on to lead them in the right direction.

I was invested and I worked hard. I wrote Bible Studies, planned events, delivered messages, recruited kids to go to retreats and camps, and even took 22 eighth-graders on a weeklong trip in RVs!

Along the way, Hannah was born in 2000, and Haley in 2002. Kristin turned Geneva's winless women's soccer team into a national contender.

But here's the real truth: All of my focus was outward. My time, energy, and commitments were all directed toward others. I was burning the candle on both ends. In public, I was an enthusiastic, energetic local youth guy. In private, I was short-tempered, tired, and frazzled. The only time I ever opened my Bible was to prepare to teach it to others. The only time I ever prayed was when I was leading others in prayer.

It wasn't that I didn't think those things were important for me to do. It just felt like what I was doing with or for others was enough.

true stories

About five years in, I started becoming more and more aware that I was living a sort of double-life. Not the kind of double-life where I was involved in some salacious activity that I was keeping secret, but the kind where everything I was teaching and preaching weren't actually connected with what I was practicing.

As I once heard someone say, "You've got to smoke what you are selling," OK, maybe that's a bad example. But it does describe what was happening in my life.

The word "burnout" definitely describes where I was headed, and I remember the exact moment when it finally hit me square in the face.

It was the fall of 2003, and I had recruited a bus full of high school kids to go on a weekend retreat. The Friday afternoon of the event had arrived, and I packed my duffle bag for the trip. As I headed out the door of our apartment to walk across the street to the waiting bus, I felt overwhelmed with a sense of dread. I turned to Kristin, "I don't want to go."

Stunned, she tried to encourage me. "It's gonna be great." But I knew that she knew what was really going on in my soul. My tank was empty.

I shed a couple of tears, honestly, wiped them away, and mustered up the courage to power through the weekend ahead.

Despite where my heart was, I am confident that God still worked in the lives of those students.

But it was a turning point.

I came home from the weekend, ready to quit. Ready for a reset. Ready to not be a fake anymore.

But how? What was the next step? Where could we go to take a break, reassess, and start a new chapter?

I researched and talked to friends and mentors. I looked online. Finally, I came across a program through an outfit called Youth With A Mission, or YWAM. I had heard of YWAM, but only knew a little bit about it. I figured they were a mission group made up of mainly young people, since the word "youth" was indeed part of their name. I didn't know much else.

The specific program within YWAM was called a Crossroads Discipleship Training School. It consisted of three months of learning about the nature and character of God while living in community, followed by two months serving somewhere in the world. YWAM had several places where this program was offered in the U.S. and around the world. After a little more research, I found one that I thought might be just the spot for Kristin and me to take our young girls for this five-month adventure: Hawaii.

It turned out that YWAM's biggest training site was in Kona on the Big Island. How convenient!

All joking aside, I had a real sense that this would be the next step. This would be the season of rest and renewal.

Kristin and I talked about it. We were scared and a bit hesitant. It's not exactly easy to tell family and friends and people in your town that you are burnt out and need to spend some time getting restored in Hawaii and doing mission work.

But that's exactly what we did. I submitted my resignation to the church. We reached out to our contacts and network and were fortunate to be able to raise the necessary funding for the journey. We got on a plane, and flew from Pittsburgh to L.A. to Kona, with a two-year-old and three-year-old in tow.

The next three months were like peeling back the layers of an onion. It was both restful and exhausting. We lived in one room, the four of us. We ate meals in community with people from over 40 countries. Hannah attended a pre-school on the campus where she was the only child who spoke English as her native language. Haley slept most nights in our bed as we couldn't let her crying disturb our neighbors sleep.

But we also were surrounded by people, who like us, were at a crossroads: burnt out or just hanging on by a thread, and ready to explore whatever the next chapter of life God was leading them into.

We listened and learned, we rested, we talked about tough things, we parented, and we prayed. It was both challenging and encouraging. For the first time in almost a decade, I felt like a human being rather than a human doing.

Oh, and our two months of learning and training in Kona was followed by two months of serving a local Maori community in Auckland, New Zealand. I know, suffering for the Lord, right? It wasn't easy, by any means, but spending that time in New Zealand was the experience of a lifetime.

The rest and renewal we were able to gain has helped to fuel us for the two decades that followed.

Throughout that time, I came back over and over again to the promise of Jesus:

Matthew 11: 28-30
"Come to me, all you who are weary and burdened, and I will give you rest. Take my yoke upon you and learn from me, for I am gentle and humble in heart, and you will find rest for your souls. For my yoke is easy and my burden is light."

Another translation of the Bible says it in words that resonated with me even more:

"Are you tired? Worn out? Burned out on religion?
Come to me. Get away with me and you'll recover your life. I'll show you how to take a real rest.
Walk with me and work with me—watch how I do it.
Learn the unforced rhythms of grace.
I won't lay anything heavy or ill-fitting on you.
Keep company with me and you'll learn to live freely and lightly."
- from The Message

Read that again.

There is a good chance that at some point in life we will all "hit the wall." It takes on many forms , but everyone reaches a season when it's time to hit the "reset" button.

When that time comes, it's important to do whatever it takes to get the rest and renewal that is needed. And, just as importantly, to take Jesus up on his offer to find that rest in Him. What exactly does that mean?

It means embracing the reality of being loved and accepted by God, through Jesus, just as we are. No presenting of our best self, no trying to impress God (or others) with some idealized version of who we think we need to be.

The radical claim of Jesus, as his friend John says in his Gospel, is that his life was "God in the flesh." He lived the life that we can't. He brought into the world the ultimate example of what it is to be a human being.

When we embrace that reality and focus on that relationship, our desire to perform and need to be accepted by others fades away. We can wake up each morning, take a deep breath, and BE. We are accepted. We don't have anything to prove. We can rest.

Since those YWAM days, I still at times slip back into the external-to-internal way of life, but more often I am living life from the inside-out.

May you learn what it means to be someone who puts a sense of being before a sense of doing, and may you have the courage to find rest for your soul in the one place where it is truly possible: the embracing, unconditional love of Jesus.

true stories

green sand beach

Our three months in Hawaii wasn't exactly a luxury vacation. Our days were filled with attending classes, meal prep and clean up, and looking after our two young children.

Haley turned two just a few days after we arrived on the Big Island, and Hannah was almost four.

Kids that age need a lot of attention, and it was all that we could handle! We lived together in one dormitory-style room: Kristin and I sleeping on a "king-size" bed that was actually two single beds pushed together, Hannah on a small twin, while Haley had a pack-n-play, although she ended up in our bed most nights. We were "roughing it" for sure, but if there is one place that you'd prefer to live simply, it would have to be Hawaii, right?

Without a car, we were mainly stuck at the YWAM base and anywhere that we could walk to in the village of Kailua-Kona.

About a month into our time there my parents were kind enough to get us a small rental car for two weeks. It was a blessing for sure!

This gave us the chance to explore more of the island, from the beaches to the volcanoes to the mountains. We soon discovered that the Big Island had a wide variety of climates, landscapes, and natural wonders.

We started our adventures by heading up the Kohala Coast. Our first stop was a small, unmarked beach called Kukio. The lagoon-like crystal clear swimming area was perfect for our young girls. We swam and played and watched the giant sea turtles bask in the sun on the rocky reef.

We ventured further north, cutting across the plains of Waimea and over to the eastern coast, then up the east coast to see the amazing views of Waipi'o Valley.

By the time we got back to our small apartment, the girls were sound asleep. We carried them inside and anticipated a solid night of rest.

Before getting to Hawaii I had worked at a church for almost 10 years, so for the first time in a long time Sunday morning meant sleeping in for as long as the girls would allow us to, so that's what we did.

But we also only had the rental car for a couple of weeks, so about mid-morning we loaded them up for another day of exploration.

We decided to drive down Route 11 towards the southern part of the island to see the Hawaii Volcanoes National Park. The girls were wiped from the previous day, so a day in the double stroller walking along the wooden-planked trails and through the lava tubes seemed like a perfect idea.

It was a typical beautiful Hawaii morning, warm and sunny. About an hour into the drive, there was a sign on the side of the road:

"SOUTHERN MOST POINT IN THE USA, 12 MILES. →"

true stories

I couldn't resist.

This is definitely one way that Kristin and I are different. She likes to know what's coming; she's not a big fan of surprises or unplanned activities.

I, on the other hand, usually fly by the seat of my pants. When I see a sign like that, I'm turning and seeing what's at the end of those 12 miles.

So that's what we did.

Some of life's best and most memorable experiences happen when we take a detour from our plans.

The small two-lane road wound its way down through the mainly desolate landscape. The only vehicles that we saw were Jeeps or trucks. Soon the pavement became less-than-well maintained, then only semi-paved. The rental car kicked up dirt all around us, so we put up the windows and blasted the AC.

By this time, Haley was asleep in her carseat, but Hannah's 3-year-old patience was wearing thin.

"Where's the lava tunnels?" her little voice questioned.

"Almost there" I promised, even though I had no idea what was at the end of the "South Point" road.

After thirty minutes or so, the road ended at a small parking lot. No markings. No signs. And no sign of a beach. Just a few cars and SUVs and a view of the ocean in the distance.

"Great job" Kristin said sarcastically, "Now what?"

There had to be more to it, I thought.

We were about to turn around when a dirt-covered Jeep carrying two younger couples emerged from the dirt path off to the side of the parking lot.

I lowered the car's window, "Aloha" I said, "Where are you guys coming from?"

"The green sand beach," replied one of the guys.

"Green sand beach?"

"Yeah, it's down this road," he said back.

Road? It didn't look like a road. He could see the perplexed look on my face.

"Well, it's not really a road. Not in that car. 4-wheel-drive only. It's not too far. Southern most point in the USA. And totally worth it."

"And there's really a green sand beach?" I wondered out loud.

"Yep. It's very cool."

"Thanks," I replied, putting up the window to keep the air conditioning from escaping anymore than it already had.

I pulled the car into a parking spot. Kristin looked at me as if to say 'What are you doing?'

"Honey, we've come this far, and you heard them. They said it's not too far. We can walk from here."

"Um" she motioned to the back seat, "We can, but the girls don't even have bathing suits and we are all wearing flip flops. We aren't exactly equipped for a hike."

"Where's the lava tunnels?" came Hannah's voice once again from behind me.

"Change of plans, Hannah." I declared confidently. "The girls can walk and if we need to we, I mean, *I* can carry them."

Kristin gave me that look again.

"It'll be fine," I insisted.

If we wait until we have all of the right equipment for the journey, we'll never take the first step. Sometimes you just have to make do with what you've got on hand in the moment.

With that, we grabbed a couple of beach towels that we'd left in the car from the day before, unloaded the girls from the back seat and covered them with sunscreen, and started our hike to the mythical green sand beach.

It was around noon when we began our trek. For about the first five minutes both girls actually walked. Haley, having just turned 2 about a month earlier, was the first to extend her little arms up to me, "Carry, daddy" she boldly requested.

I lifted her onto my hip and trudged along, my flip flops sliding on the sandy path.

Every so often, either from in front of us or from behind, a truck or Jeep would approach and we would have to step off to the side of the trail/path/road.

It wasn't long before Hannah's request to be carried was heard. I passed Haley over to Kristin, and heaved Hannah up onto my shoulders. I could feel the sweat dripping down the center of my back.

The trail wound along the coast, at times turning toward the ocean, only to then weave back north so that the water would be behind us. No green sand beach in sight.

After about an hour, we decided to take a rest on the side of the trail. We drank a few sips of water from one of the couple of bottles that we'd brought with us. Kristin suggested that maybe we should turn around. Unlike me, she was thinking ahead, remembering that every step forward on this hike was making the hike back that much longer. A Jeep approached from in front of us and I waved it down.

"How much farther until the green sand beach?" I asked.

"Just a few more minutes," said the guy in the passenger seat, "and then the hike down."

The what? Hike down?

I convinced Hannah to hop off my shoulders and finish the hike like a "big girl."

Finally, as the sound of crashing waves grew closer, the trail snaked towards the edge of a ravine, and what we saw in front of us was stunning.

It was what we'd been waiting for: the southernmost beach in the United States, carved into an inlet ravine, and the sand did indeed have a greenish color.

The toughest part of the journey still lay before us: descending down the rugged rocks to the sandy shore. There was no specific path, so we had to make our way down whatever way we could.

Our brave little girls followed our lead and very carefully and slowly, the four of us managed to climb down.

When we made it to the shoreline, we found about 30 other people there: all at least young adults or older. They looked at us like we were crazy for bringing such small children.

The Green Sand Beach was honestly the most amazing place that I have ever been on this planet. The color of the sand, the blue water, and the rocky cliffs rising up on both sides of the nearly 100-foot long beachfront. Do a Google image search of "big island green sand beach." The pictures that show up will only do a slight justice to how unique and spectacular it is.

The girls played at the edge of the water as Kristin and me relaxed on our towels. We were having such a nice time in this otherworldly location that we didn't think much about the climb out of the ravine or the hike back.

Soon, the sun began dropping in the sky to the west, so we packed up our few belongings and began the strenuous climb up the rocks and back to the path. By this time Hannah and Haley were worn out, and I anticipated the hike back would be much longer than the trip in.

true stories

As we began walking, it was clear that Hannah and Haley were going to need to be carried. Neither Kristin nor I was excited about the prospect of carrying these little humans for the long walk back to the car.

I told myself that they were going to walk as far as they could before the carrying began, so that's what I told them. Nice work. Dad of the year.

But then, I had an idea. Many of the other people at the beach that day had driven their 4-wheel drive vehicles.

It was time to hitchhike.

So when the next small pickup truck approached heading in the same direction as we were, I faced it as we stepped to the side of the road/trail, and stuck out my thumb. I tried to make the expression on my face a perfect mixture of kindness and desperation.

They passed by us without even slowing down. This happened two or three more times. So much for island hospitality!

That's when I heard Hannah's little voice from near my knees,

"Dad, we should pray that God sends a nice person to pick us up."

"Great idea Hannah. In fact, since you had the idea, how about you say the prayer."

"OK," she said, pausing. She closed her eyes and clenched her little hands together in a serious prayer pose.

"God, please help us. We are tired. Please send a nice person to pick us up and take us back to our car. Amen."

Within a matter of seconds, a Jeep came into view. I picked Hannah up and sat her on my hip. We both stuck out our thumbs as far as we could. The Jeep slowed down and came to a stop, and an older gentleman who was driving spoke,

"Wanna squeeze in?"

A woman sat in the passenger seat next to him, and another older couple was in the back seat.

"Are you sure?" I said, seeing little room for our family of four.

"You bet," he cheerfully replied.

The woman in the back seat climbed into the front seat and pressed in close to her friend. The man who remained in the back seat pushed the door open, and the four of us squeezed into the Jeep, Kristin and I each with a girl on our laps.

The eight of us chatted during the 20-minute ride back to the parking lot, where we unloaded and thanked them for their kindness.

The sun was setting over the expansive ocean while we drove back to Kona. Both girls instantly fell asleep in the back seat as Kristin and I talked about what a great unexpected adventure we'd just experienced.

That evening, as we were putting them to bed, I asked Hannah what her favorite part of the weekend was: Kukio beach? Waimea? Waipi'o Valley? The green sand beach?

"When God answered my prayer," she said confidently.

From the mouth of babes, right?

It was an amazing reminder that even in the midst of a simple thing like a hike, she had seen a clear and direct answer to her prayer.

That's not always how prayer works. Sometimes we pray and the immediate response is...nothing. Sometimes we pray and we don't even think to check to see if or how our prayer was answered.

But there are also those times when we pray and we have the privilege of seeing or experiencing a clear answer right away. We have to recognize and remember these times. They build faith. They embolden us to keep praying.

For Hannah that day, she spoke words. Simple, bold, direct words of a prayer. And within her lens of experience, those words aligned with God's plans for us, and it built her faith.

Most of us, when we encounter the next hurdle or bump or rough patch, tend to complain or blame or moan or panic. What if we prayed? What if we spoke simple, direct words to God.

Jesus had a lot to say about this. Here is my personal favorite passage. It gives insight into Jesus' understanding of prayer.

Matthew 7:7-11
Ask, and it will be given to you; seek, and you will find; knock, and it will be opened to you. For everyone who asks receives, and the one who seeks finds, and to the one who knocks it will

be opened. Or which one of you, if his son asks him for bread, will give him a stone? Or if he asks for a fish, will give him a serpent? If you then, who are evil, know how to give good gifts to your children, how much more will your Father who is in heaven give good things to those who ask him!

My summary of that passage goes like this:
Be like Hannah. If it's on your heart, it's on God's heart. He's a good God. He cares. He is waiting for you to ask him, just like a dad waits for a child to ask for a simple gift. It might not come in the timing or way that you expect.

On that day in 2004, God seemed to reply to the prayer in a moment. That's not always going to happen.

I really like a portion of this prayer that is part of the Anglican prayer tradition, written by John Chrysostom:

"Fulfill now, O Lord, our desires and petitions as may be best for us..."

That's a wonderful line, isn't it? It shows that we can pray and trust that God has our best in mind. In fact, he knows much better than we do.

Through serious troubles and small challenges that we all will face, we have a chance to learn to talk to God. May our prayers be like Hannah's was that day! God is waiting to hear from us. Give prayer a try.

true stories

joyful noise

Back in the 1990s, when you were a youth pastor at a large suburban church, there were certain gifts and talents that you were expected to possess. In my early twenties, I fit the profile almost perfectly.

Outgoing...check.
Fun...check.
A good communicator...check.
Able to plan events...check.
A little crazy...check.
Good at playing the acoustic guitar and leading kids in singing...not so much!

I was so close! While I really did possess traits that made me a good fit for someone working with kids in the context of such a church, my musical ability was severely lacking.

But I felt obligated to fit the mold, so I purchased an acoustic guitar and attempted to teach myself how to play it. Even tuning it was a struggle. Here is a tip - if you can't tune an acoustic guitar without the aid of a guitar tuner, that might be an indication that you aren't a musically gifted person. And I mean I wasn't even close to being able to do this. I would play the low "E" string, and think to myself, yes that sounds about right. Then I would turn on my guitar tuner and discover that what I thought sounded "about right" was off by at least a whole note.

But I was committed. A youth pastor in the 1990s who didn't play guitar and lead music? Unthinkable!

My bony fingers struggled to find the correct strings, and despite having a good sense of rhythm, I found strumming the strings and moving from chord to chord to be an incredible challenge.

Nevertheless, I persisted. After several months, I had taught myself a few simple three-chord progressions (which really was all that you needed to play most "youth group" songs). I had even managed to figure out how to sing and play at the same time, although the sound coming from my vocal chords could hardly be called singing.

I am not totally tone deaf. My musical ear can, for the most part, tell what is "on key" and what isn't. And I could tell that my singing was not matching the sound of the chords coming from my guitar when I played. The guitar sounded fine. My voice didn't.

But I would sit in my office at the church most mornings and practice for a good 30 or 40 minutes.

Meanwhile, my boss at the time, Patrick, was incredibly gifted in music. He could play. He could sing. He could harmonize. He could perform. Heck, he graduated from the theater department at Carnegie Mellon University!

Each week at the church, on Wednesday mornings, there was a special group of people that would gather in the sanctuary for a worship service. A dear woman in the congregation, Nanky, had started a ministry for adults with special needs. 30-50 of them would gather together, along with their caregivers, for the Joyful Noise service. These were adults with severe mental and physical challenges, many of them wheelchair bound and unable to verbalize, yet this service was a special time for them each week.

Patrick was not only musically gifted, but he had a servant's heart, and each week he would lead the music, alongside Nanky, at the Joyful Noise service. I remember walking into the back of the sanctuary on a couple of occasions and seeing the two of them up front, Patrick singing and playing guitar, and Nanky leading the singing with him, even though many in the audience seemed unaware of what was going on.

I talked with Patrick about this, and he shared that, even though the people at the service had special needs and didn't really sing along, he could tell that the music was a ministry to them.

One Wednesday morning about six months into my time on staff, I was sitting in my office practicing my guitar and there was a knock on the door. It was Nanky.

"Patrick called me this morning. He's really sick and can't make it. Do you think that you would be able to fill in for him this morning at the Joyful Noise service?"

Sweet Nanky, who had started the service because she herself had a daughter with special needs, stood at the door to my office. How could I say no? Well, actually, I tried.

"Oh my," I said, "I am sorry to hear that. Honestly, I am just learning how to play the guitar and can only play a couple of songs. I wish I could help."

"Well, what songs do you know to play?" she asked.

I mentioned a couple of youth group songs that I was pretty sure that she wouldn't know. I also happened to mention "Amazing Grace."

"Well that is terrific," she said, "we can just limit it to one song, and we will do that one. Can you meet me in the front of the sanctuary at 9:50?"

"Um, yes, of course. Sounds great."

So there I was, in my office, frantically practicing the 3-chord progression for "Amazing Grace."

Here's the thing: In the late 1990s, there was a 'youth group' version of the song, with an updated melody and a chorus of "Alleluia"s. That was the version that I (sort-of) knew how to play, so that's what I practiced. Nanky, I would later find out, was not aware of this new melody.

As the clock ticked to 9:50, I walked from my office down the hallway to the sanctuary. People were arriving, most of them in specially-equipped vans, and were being escorted by their aides into the building.

Nanky stood at the front of the aisles and watched me approach, guitar slung over my shoulder.

I began to sweat. I could feel my armpits and lower back dampening with beads of moisture. This is not going to turn out well, I thought.

After the sanctuary was totally full, Nanky and I stood together at the podium, sharing the microphone that was perched on top. My acoustic guitar didn't have an electric hook-up, so it would have to be played without any amplification.

Nanky welcomed everyone and let them know that I was going to be helping lead the music, and that this morning there was just going to be one song, "Amazing Grace."

She turned to me and indicated that I should begin the song. I looked out at the audience and smiled, noticing that most of the special needs audience seemed to be only partially aware of what was happening up front.

I started my chord progression, and it didn't take long to realize that Nanky and I were not on the same page. While I was playing the updated youth group melody, she was about to begin singing the old, traditional hymn. And she did.

We were totally out of sync. The guitar and the vocals didn't go together AT ALL. But Nanky sang and smiled at me. She was so gracious. It seemed, to me, like a disaster, but her joyful spirit and enthusiasm were unwavering.

And the people there, they didn't mind at all. I heard some attempt to sing along, while others simply verbalized their praise in whatever way they could manage. Many were unable to sing, but smiled widely and swayed back and forth in their wheelchairs.

We struggled through the verses and chorus, but as the song came to a close, the room was not only filled with disjointed music, it was filled with a joyful noise.

Nanky gave me a pat on the back, and I walked and sat down in the front row. She then led the group through some prayers, and invited one of the caregivers up front to share a short sermon of encouragement.

I will never forget that morning. In spite of my total lack of musical ability, there was a presence of God in the room that could not be denied.

The words of Paul in Romans 8, verse 26, became vividly true that day:

In the same way, the Spirit helps us in our weakness. We do not know what we ought to pray for, but the Spirit himself intercedes for us through wordless groans.

The people in that room taught me that even when my words or guitar chords seem out of sync or out of tune, God still hears. Even the name of the service itself was a reminder that it's the heart of worship that matters, not the beauty of the singing or the perfect playing of an instrument.

Psalm 100:2 says,
Worship the Lord with gladness; come before him with joyful songs.

That's what happened that day, and it has served as a reminder to me that it is impossible to be a 'worshiper' and a 'worship critic' at the same time. God isn't like a judge on American Idol or The Voice. Psalm 22:3 says that he "inhabits" the praises of his people. This means that God shows up in a special way when we simply open our mouths and acknowledge God for who God is.

Now, almost 25 years after I "led" worship at the Joyful Noise service, I am a retired guitar player. But I am not retired from making a joyful noise. That will remain a lifelong endeavor.

So no matter if you are singing an old hymn with an old melody or the latest song from a trendy worship band, it's a chance to give praise to the amazing grace of a God who deserves every Alleluia.

true stories

the (stroller) walk of shame

As a young dad and sports fanatic, I enthusiastically signed my kids up for every organized sports activity that was offered.

And I was a little crazy. Or maybe a lot crazy. I was the dad yelling from the sidelines at my kids, at other people's kids, and yes, at the refs or officials. Thinking back, it makes me cringe. I was *that* guy.

But my immature sideline antics began way before my kids even started playing sports.

My wife Kristin started her first position as a head coach of a women's college soccer team right after she herself graduated from college. Her first season, while we were dating before we got married, she was just 22 and only a few months older than the oldest players on her team.

And I was the #1 fan. I attended almost every game, home or away. I cheered. I yelled at the refs. I even dabbled in harassing the players on the other team.

After five years of building a successful college program, Kristin, wanting to spend more time with our growing family, transitioned to a new role as the Head Coach of our local high school girls team. The team had talented players, and she was a great coach. And once again, I was there, in the bleachers, at every game, being that guy.

Many times, our car rides home were quite unpleasant, because they included her expressing to me some degree of embarrassment for my spectator behavior. I would apologize and promise to do better. But inevitably I would repeat the same obnoxious antics at the next game.

This continued even when we had Haley, our second daughter. I would attend the games with our daughters, pushing three-year-old Hannah and one-year-old Haley in the double stroller. I tried to keep them occupied so that I could focus on what was happening on the field, ready to let any game official know when they'd fallen short of my high expectations.

My barbs towards the refs weren't mean. I didn't swear or call them names. In fact, just the opposite. I majored in sarcasm, humor, and pointed critique. Rather than, "Hey ref, you suck!," I steered more towards things like, "Sir, you can't make an accurate call from that far away. These players are running. You should be too!"

Under most circumstances the word "sir" would indicate respect, but when partnered with sarcasm and criticism, does the opposite. Here is another example:

"Sir, offsides is determined by where the player was when the ball was played, not when it was received. I know, it can be confusing. Try to keep up."

Ouch.

One particular weekday afternoon it all came crashing down.

true stories

Kristin's team had an away game at a nearby school. It was a venue that I had never been to before, and the opponent would be one that her team was far superior to.

I got Hannah and Haley situated in the car and folded up our double stroller, loading it into the back. We drove to the game, singing along to the Wiggles.

When we arrived, I was surprised to see that the game was not being played on the main stadium at the high school, but on a nearby practice field. The field was surrounded by a fence, with the team benches on the far sideline. There were no bleachers; just a narrow space between the near sideline and the fence, where parents were standing or sitting in lawn chairs that they had brought with them.

There was only one entry/exit point to the parking lot: a gate at the end of the field.

I walked in, wheeling the girls in the double stroller, down to the far end of the field, where most of the parents of our team had settled in for the game.

Hannah asked to get down from the stroller. With so little space between the fence and the field, I hesitated to let an active three-year-old have the freedom to be anywhere other than strapped into her seat, but I relented, allowing her to get out and stand next to me.

The game began. Surprisingly, it was a much more competitive match that I had anticipated. Matters were not helped by the fact that the refs were clearly favoring the other team, allowing them to get away with rough fouls and making some terrible calls against our team. I tried to control myself, realizing that my close proximity to the field and to the other spectators would make me very noticeable to the officials, and anyone else for that matter.

Finally, about 25 minutes into the first half, Kristin's team scored. That was quickly followed by another goal, then a third. As the first half came to close, they held a comfortable lead, in spite of the refs who were clearly doing all that they could to favor the home team.

"Can I go say hi to mommy?"

Hannah asked me this question at halftime of just about every game. And because the team usually held a comfortable edge on the scoreboard, I would allow her to run across the field and visit Kristin and the players.

"OK, but make sure that you come back when I call over to you."

Off she went, sprinting the width of the field. Several of the players greeted her as she made it to them, and Kristin picked her up and gave her a big hug.

Haley had grown restless in the stroller, and so I reached in to pick her up. That's when it hit me: the familiar scent of a dirty diaper. I looked up at the halftime clock, seeing that there were only seven minutes left until the end of the break. In my haste to make it to the game on time, I had left the diaper bag in the car. While I am not a perfect dad, I knew that leaving her in her poopy diaper for the whole 40-minute second half of the game was a bad idea, so I made the move, walking briskly down the sideline and out of the gate, pushing the stroller through the parking lot to the car.

I performed an efficient diaper change, loaded Haley back into the stroller, and headed back into the fenced-in field to watch the second half.

It was at this point that I realized that Hannah was still with the team on the far side of the field. The players were on the field to warm up, so it wasn't smart or safe for her to run straight across.

As I arrived back at my spot across from the bench, the second half was about to start. Kristin waved her arms at me and then pointed to Hannah, sitting on the bench with the substitute players, as if to say "I guess she'll just stay over here."

I told myself it was OK. It was 3-0 at half, and could have easily been 6-0 or 7-0. The ease of the game made it less of a problem that Hannah was over there with the team. No big deal, I told myself.

Play resumed and the officiating got worse. It wasn't long before the unexpected happened. The other team scored. Then, not more than two minutes later, they scored again, this time when one of their players was clearly in an offside position!

With the score now 3-2, the intensity increased, as did my frustration with the unfair advantage the refs seemed to be giving to the other team.

With about 10 minutes left, one of our players was taken down with a cleat-first tackle right in front of me, and also in clear view of the ref. He had no choice but to blow his whistle and call the foul, giving us a direct free kick, around 20 yards from the goal.

true stories

The rules of soccer state that players on the other team must stand back at least 10 yards when a direct kick is being taken. As our player prepared the ball to take the kick, there were four girls from the other team forming a "wall," as is often done. Totally fine. However, they were no more than five yards in front of our kick-taker. The ref was standing right there in front of me, watching this clear violation, and didn't do or say anything! I couldn't hold it in...

"Sir, they have to give her ten yards! She's asking for it, and you aren't doing anything. Do you know the rules, sir!?"

Then the whistle blew, and he turned around slowly to face me.

Oops.

All eyes turned in my direction. He pointed at me, then at the gate at the far end of the field.

"Young man, that's enough. Please leave."

The dad with the baby in the stroller and the three-year-old currently sitting on the team bench had just gotten booted from the game.

Mortified that I was being called out in front of everyone, I didn't say a word.

I turned and pushed the stroller, traversing the narrow space between the fence and the field, in front of ALL of the parents. After what seemed like an eternity, I reached the gate where the security guard was waiting to escort me out.

true stories

As I pushed Haley in the stroller in front of all of those parents, the referee had to pause the game as he waited until I was gone. It was humiliating.

Kristin's team held onto their lead and ended up winning, 3-2. Hannah watched from the bench. I watched from outside the gate, peering through the fence like some kind of creeper.

Needless to say, my wife wasn't exactly thrilled with me.

She brought Hannah to me as she and the team got ready to get back on the bus, not saying a word. Words weren't necessary. The look on her face spoke quite clearly.

That day was a bit of a turning point for the way that I behaved at sporting events. I mean, I haven't always been an angel since then, and my transformation isn't complete. But it's been steady progress to at least partial sanity.

To be honest, my loose tongue is still something that I struggle with almost every day. Even in my late 40s, I say so many things that I regret. I often speak at the wrong time, in the wrong place, and much more loudly than necessary.

The words that we choose to say or not say have a great effect on those around us. That day, my words got me kicked out of a soccer game and brought shame upon me and my family.

A bit in the mouth of a horse controls the whole horse. A small rudder on a huge ship in the hands of a skilled captain sets a course in the face of the strongest winds. A word out of your mouth may seem of no account, but it can accomplish nearly anything—or destroy it!

It only takes a spark to set off a forest fire. A careless or wrongly placed word out of your mouth can do that. By our speech we can ruin the world, turn harmony to chaos, throw mud on a reputation, send the whole world up in smoke and go up in smoke with it, smoke right from the pit of hell.

This is scary: You can tame a tiger, but you can't tame a tongue—it's never been done. The tongue runs wild, a wanton killer. With our tongues we bless God our Father; with the same tongues we curse the very men and women he made in his image. Curses and blessings out of the same mouth!

Did you just catch that? Those last three paragraphs weren't mine. They are from the brother of Jesus. James wrote a letter that is included in the New Testament of the Bible, and those paragraphs are from Eugene Peterson's The Message translation.

He captures the power of our words so well. The rudder of a ship. A spark that sets ablaze a whole forest. A wanton killer.

How many relationships are ruined because of hurtful words? How many friendships would be healed with a simple word of sweetness or forgiveness?

This is something that we all need to work on. I am not the only person who finds controlling my words and emotions to be a lifelong process. I bet that even as you are reading this, specific moments are easy to recall when you said something that you later wished you could take back.

But there is hope for all of us loose-tongued types. With God's help, we can learn to be, as James says earlier in his letter, "quick to listen, slow to speak and slow to become angry." We can start out as the crazy-on-the-sideline sports parent and work our way towards becoming the calm, rational, supportive person that we desire to be. It won't happen overnight, and we will still slip up from time to time.

The next time you find yourself ready to let loose or spark a fire with your words, pause, take a deep breath, and remember that there is a better way

true stories

wings over pittsburgh

Patrick Hempen was known to me as the dad of three outstanding young people in the church where I worked for almost 10 years. Both of his boys made Eagle Scout, and both attended military academies after high school. His daughter was a dedicated student as well, and had a servant's heart. Pat was a strong man, quiet but approachable. But I never actually called him by his first name. To me, he was Mr. Hempen.

At church, he volunteered as an usher and greeter. I recall that every time I saw him he greeted me with a firm handshake and the same phrase, "The patience of Job." By this, I believe he meant that to be a youth pastor, I must have patience of biblical proportions.

Mr. Hempen was a man of mystery. When I would ask his sons, Eric and Jake, what their dad did for a living, they would always answer very vaguely.

"Something with the government. I think."

"I'm not really sure. He doesn't talk much about it. I think he works for the military."

"CIA, FBI, FAA. I think he works for one of those. Maybe all three."

A tall man with short gray-black hair and a chiseled jawline, Mr. Hempen looked like he could have been Tom Skerret's stand-in for Top Gun.

One day as I was leaving the church service, he stopped me in the lobby and asked me what my plans were for the upcoming Saturday. This took me by surprise, but I figured if he was recruiting me for some covert government operation, I better step up for my country.

"I think I am all clear this Saturday."

"Great," he replied, "I have some hours to complete at the aviation club. I'd love to take you up in the Cessna."

"That would be amazing! I'd love to." I confirmed.

"Terrific, I will pick you up at 0700 sharp."

"Yes sir," I replied almost instinctively.

I'd flown as a passenger on a commercial airplane many times in my life, but I'd never been in an aircraft as small as a Cessna. I was looking forward to it, but I'd be lying if I said I wasn't a little nervous as well.

Saturday arrived, and Mr. Hempen was outside of our apartment at 7 AM, waiting for me in his Prius.

We drove out to the aviation club, which was about 30 minutes away. He asked me about what airplanes I had ever been in, and I explained that I'd only flown on commercial jets. He let me know that this would be much different. "This," he explained, "is real flying. There is nothing like it."

We arrived at the small county airport, and waiting for us in a small hangar was the Cessna. It was a small aircraft, with just room for the pilot and co-pilot. It was a prop-plane, meaning that it was powered by one single propeller attached to the front end.

Mr. Hempen grabbed the appropriate clipboard and began to go through the extensive pre-flight safety checklist and protocol. He checked every facet of the plane at least three times, making sure that everything was exactly as it should be.

He handed me a pair of flying gloves, and helped me climb into the co-pilot spot. He made his way to the pilot seat, and we both connected our headsets, the final step as we readied for the flight.

I noticed that there were duplicate piloting controls both in front of him and in front of me, while on his side there were an array of indicators, dials, and switches.

After checking and adjusting various knobs and buttons, Mr. Hempen turned on his headset.

"Check, check," he said over the headsets.

"I can hear you," I replied, not exactly sure if that was the right response, or if he was even talking to me.

"Alright, here we go."

Next, he spoke some technical flying jargon to the person working the control tower, and we taxied out to a spot at the end of the runway. It was a beautiful spring day, with a light breeze and barely a cloud in the sky.

We sped down the runway, and then he pulled back on the yoke. We ascended quickly into the sky, and the view from the small cockpit gave me the feeling that I was actually flying. Unlike a big airplane, it felt more like being a passenger on a very large bird.

We banked to the left, then slightly back to the right as we flew higher and higher.

"We'll take a nice trip up here and then head down towards the city," he informed me.

From our aerial vantage point, I noticed just how much of the western Pennsylvania landscape was woods, and I could also pick out several familiar landmarks on the ground below us. Yes, I could write something here about how important it is to gain a new perspective. Something about how it is helpful to zoom out from the daily struggles and see things in the bigger picture. But there actually was something about the trip yet to come and would teach me a much greater lesson.

We cruised around a bit and then he pointed the aircraft towards downtown Pittsburgh.

Once we got close to the city, Mr. Hempen started talking in detailed pilot lingo to someone on the other side of the in-cabin radio. I heard what sounded like information about our location and a request for "clearance" and "permission granted."

As we approached the city, we flew what seemed like just a few hundred feet above the ground. First, we circled over Heinz Field, home of the Steelers, and PNC Park, the Pirates baseball stadium. Mr. Hempen carefully banked the airplane so that I could get a great view from my co-pilot window.

Next, we turned toward Point State Park, gliding above the confluence of the Monongahela and Allegheny Rivers. We rose sharply, then turned, once again leaning the plane for a great view of the city skyline.

Finally, we headed to our final landmark, the Cathedral of Learning at the University of Pittsburgh. The large Gothic revival cathedral is the tallest education building in the western hemisphere.

I was sure that our amazingly up close aerial tour of the city was only because of Mr. Hempen's status within whatever government agency or entity he happened to work for. I was not only in the hands of an experienced pilot, but one with flying privileges that exceeded the norm.

After the birds-eye tour of these Pittsburgh landmarks, he turned the plane and we headed north, about to begin the flight back to the airstrip that we'd taken off from about 20 minutes earlier.

That's when Mr. Hempen spoke two words that I wasn't expecting to hear: "Your turn."

He motioned for me to take control of the co-pilot yoke. I reached out and placed my hands on the left and right of the controls.

"It's quite simple. Turn it to the left to go left. Turn it right to go right. Pull back to ascend, and push forward to descend. Ready?"

true stories

He took his hands off of the yoke in front of him and folded his arms across his chest.

When the day started, I had been extremely nervous about going for a ride in such a small aircraft, and now I wasn't just a passenger - I was flying a freaking airplane.

I pulled back and we slowly ascended, and then I steered left and we turned slightly, following the Ohio River below as it wound through the landscape.

Mr. Hempen didn't give me step by step instructions, but he did chime in with coaching, reminding me to be mindful of the horizon, and showing me on the instrument panel where to look to get a gauge on my flight angles.

He let me fly the Cessna most of the way back to the aviation club. As we got close, he took back the controls and guided us safely down, landing smoothly on the pavement, barely a sound made as the plane's wheels touched the ground.

It was one of those unexpected experiences that I will never forget. I gained a new perspective on the city where I'd grown up, having now seen it in a way that I never had before.

But once we were on the ground, it occurred to me that although I had the sensation of flying the plane, there was never actually a time during our flight when Mr. Hempen wasn't in complete control.

Yes, he allowed me to steer. Yes, my hands were on the yoke while he rested his. But that was somewhat deceptive. He still maintained the speed of the aircraft, and at any moment, he could have taken over, using his vast experience and expertise to keep us safe.

My hands were on the controls, but he was actually still piloting the plane.

The experience was a reminder to me that when it comes to the "flight" of my life, God is ultimately the one in control. Yes, he allows me to take the yoke, to steer, to bank to the left and to the right. But in the end, I am not the pilot. He is.

Proverbs 3:5-6 says
Trust in the Lord with all your heart and lean not on your own understanding; in all your ways acknowledge him, and he will make your paths straight.

This doesn't mean that we are supposed to sit around and do nothing. There is a time when we hear a voice say very clearly: 'Your turn." We have our "ways." We have our "path." It's a reminder that on our journey, on the path that we take, we also must learn to trust, to acknowledge that we don't have as much control, at times, as we might hope. But also trust that the pilot knows what he is doing and has our best interest in mind.

The Message translation rephrases it like this:
Trust God from the bottom of your heart;
Don't try to figure out everything on your own.
Listen for God's voice in everything you do, everywhere you go; he's the one who will keep you on track.

Whether you are in a season of soaring, just getting off the ground, or unsure if you are taking the correct flight angle, acknowledge that God is the real pilot. Trust the one who is ultimately in control.

true stories

swept away in costa rica

The day spent playing soccer at the prison in Costa Rica (see the chapter "cai jorge debravo") was so impactful, but the whole trip wasn't as exciting or eventful as that day.

In fact, the main work project that our team did was much more mundane. We worked with a local church to help them upgrade their meeting space. They had recently upgraded their seating from plastic lawn chairs to wooden benches, and we spent three straight days sanding and staining the benches.

I wanted to make sure that I set a good example, so I worked just as hard as anyone on our team, sanding and sanding and sanding.

The pastor we worked with was named Pastor Miguel. He and I bonded quickly and had many good conversations. Since I was the leader, he was always checking in with me, to make sure that our team had everything that was needed and was having a good experience.

As we approached lunchtime on the third day of sanding the benches, I took a water break and was standing off to the side, stretching my back, which was sore from hours of bending over for our work. I was also feeling the stress of leading our team, dealing with the different personalities, expectations, and dynamics of the group. My pain was physical, and it was also mental. I was stressed.

Pastor Miguel saw me standing there, and came over to ask me what was wrong. I let him know that I was fine, and that I was just having a bit of soreness in my back.

"Pastor Mark," he said, "I don't want this to be a burden to you. Please, follow me, and I will help you."

I wasn't sure what was going to happen next, but Pastor Miguel was in charge. He walked ahead of me, out the door of the church and turned left, down the sidewalk along the busy city street. He was moving briskly, and I just followed along. After a couple of blocks, we turned again, then crossed the street, and traveled down a few more blocks.

Suddenly, as we came around a corner, he opened a door for me, and I stepped inside a building. I didn't even have time to see where we had arrived, but as soon as I entered, I noticed the sign on the wall: Inara Estetica & Spa

He'd brought me to a spa.

He followed me in and was warmly greeted by the receptionist, and in Spanish he explained to her who I was and that he had brought me here because my back was hurt. I thought I heard him say something to her that sounded like "one hour."

He then turned to me and said, "Pastor Mark, they will give your back relief for one hour. I will be back to get you then."

So, yep. While the rest of the team, including my wife and 8-year-old daughter Hannah, were busy sanding the benches back at the church, I was going to be getting a one-hour massage. Not only that, but I had disappeared without any warning or explanation.

I followed a tall, strong, broad-shouldered woman back to one of the spa rooms. I am built like a distance runner, and this lady was built like a linebacker. I prayed that she wouldn't break me.

I went into the room and she waited outside. I'd been wearing a typical summer outfit: a t-shirt, shorts, socks, and athletic shoes. As I began to undress. I made the decision to keep my shorts on. I wasn't sure if this was the normal protocol for a massage, but undressing any further felt a bit too awkward!

I sat down on the massage table, facing the door. Then, a gentle knock, and I said, "Come in."

The masseuse entered, and asked me where I was in pain the most, but she was speaking in Spanish, so I couldn't really understand what she was saying. I motioned to my neck, shoulders and lower back. She nodded that she understood, and motioned for me to lie face down.

For the next hour this strong Costa Rican woman worked my back with a series of squeezes and jabs that made my eyes water, but of course I had to lie there and not let on that I was in any pain. Slowly, however, I felt much of the soreness and tension in the muscles of my back begin to dissipate. As my body relaxed, so did my mind. I started to pray, and God reminded me that he was in charge of the group and that I didn't need to worry so much about pleasing everyone or meeting everyone's expectations.

The time actually flew by, and I think I may have even fallen asleep for a few minutes. She ended with a flurry of karate chops up and down my entire back, and then exited the room, indicating that my hour was up.

As I sat up to get dressed, I felt that all of the tension and pain in my back was gone. I was relaxed, free of the stress that my body had been feeling. My mind was clear and my spirit was refreshed.

I walked back into the lobby, where Pastor Miguel was waiting, a big smile on his face.

"Feeling better, Pastor Mark?" he asked

"Si, muy bien" I replied, using up about half of my Spanish vocabulary.

We exited the spa, walking into the bright sunlight of the afternoon. As we headed back to the church, I started thinking about how I was going to explain to Kristin and the rest of the group where I had been for the past hour.

We walked through the door of the church and Hannah came running up to me right away.

"Dad, where were you? Mommy was worried."

Pastor Miguel, I then realized, had not told anyone of my whereabouts. Kristin walked over with that look on her face that said, where have you been?

A few more people from the group also stopped their lunch break and joined them. I sheepishly explained to the small crowd that Pastor Miguel had taken me away, not even informing me where we were going, and that he'd treated me to a one-hour massage at a spa down the street.

The looks on their faces? Disbelief. Jealousy. Bewilderment.

Pastor Miguel was standing there, and did his best to explain in English that I was the leader and that leaders need to take care of leaders. And also said something about me being old and kind of weak. Everyone laughed.

It was such a blessing. Not something that I planned or anticipated. I learned that day that sometimes, when we least expect it, blessings come our way.

So many times, we go through our days just grinding them out, one task or one hour at a time. We can get tired, or sore, or beat down. And then, out of the blue, a blessing drops in our lap. I think that sometimes we miss these blessings because we've got our head down and aren't looking for them or even open to them happening.

As I look back on my life, I can see so many times where I've been blessed when I didn't see it coming. I have tried to live with an openhanded posture towards these kinds of events and moments.

What about you? Are you so fixated on the daily grind that you are closing yourself off from someone who may want to bless you with an unexpected gift? Are you focused on the stress, or living with an assurance that God will provide for your every need?

All I did that day in Costa Rica was listen to and follow Pastor Miguel. I didn't question or challenge or even hesitate.

There are many times in Jesus' life when unexpected blessings shift the story and show God's desire to provide for the needs of the people that he loves. With each miracle, healing, and act of kindness and compassion, Jesus shows us that God is looking to bless people, even when they least expect it.

In his longest and most famous teaching, Jesus gives great insight into the way in which we can ruin or detract from God's blessing in our lives by having the wrong mindset. Read this passage as if Jesus is talking to you about your life right now:

Matthew 6: 25-33
"Therefore I tell you, do not worry about your life, what you will eat or drink; or about your body, what you will wear. Isn't life more than food, and the body more than clothes? Look at the birds of the air; they do not sow or reap or store away in barns, and yet your heavenly Father feeds them. Are you not much more valuable than they? Can any one of you by worrying add a single hour to your life?

And why do you worry about clothes? See how the flowers of the field grow. They do not labor or spin. Yet I tell you that not even Solomon in all his splendor was dressed like one of these. If that is how God clothes the grass of the field, which is here today and tomorrow is thrown into the fire, will he not much more clothe you—you of little faith? So do not worry, saying, 'What shall we eat?' or 'What shall we drink?' or 'What shall we wear?' For the pagans run after all these things, and your heavenly Father knows that you need them. But seek first his kingdom and his righteousness, and all these things will be given to you as well."

This isn't a promise that life is going to be one blessing after another, with no tough times in between. It's an insight into how we should each approach each day. We can choose to have a mindset of worry, or we can live with expectations of blessings.

true stories

rv trip

There was a time when MTV actually showed music videos. As a teenager, I vividly remember anticipating when the world premier videos of my favorite artists would be aired. Shows like "Yo! MTV Raps" and "Alternative Nation" focused on highly-stylized video productions, and most of the programming consisted mostly of music videos.

Then, in the mid-1990s, things started to change. First, there was a game show on MTV called "Remote Control." Then, as reality TV became more popular, MTV debuted "The Real World", where this was the tagline:

"This is the true story of seven strangers picked to live in a house, work together and have their lives taped — to find out what happens when people stop being polite and start getting real."

Sometime in the late 1990s, they took "The Real World" concept on the road, literally, with a new show called "Road Rules."

The series followed five to six strangers, between the ages of 18 and 24, without any access to their own money or other resources, spending 24 hours a day living together in an RV, traveling from location to location. The strangers were guided by a set of clues and missions to complete at each destination.

true stories

When Road Rules was at the peak of its popularity, I was finishing my second year as a middle school youth pastor. I'd spent those two years in the local community, reaching out to kids and spending time with them, helping them explore faith and Jesus, and walking with them as they navigated the weirdness of 7th and 8th grade.

I was heavily invested. I volunteered in the fall as an assistant middle school girls soccer coach, in the winter as an assistant boys 8th grade basketball coach, and in the spring as one of the founding coaches of a boys middle school lacrosse team.

The impact in the community was palpable. We'd hosted middle school dances at the church as an outreach to the community and the local school district checked our schedule when planning their own dances or events, because they knew that 60-70% of the middle schoolers would be at the church on a Friday night.

Kristin and I didn't have any kids yet, so my work schedule, between coaching, church programs, retreats, and long Sundays, was super busy. I was easily working 65 hours per week, and I loved it.

As a 25 year old, I was still pretty immature in many ways, so I fit in pretty well with middle schoolers! But along with that relatability, I also brought to the table wisdom and guidance that many kids were craving.

Kristin and I developed close, mentoring relationships with many of the students. As a core group of them were about to finish 8th grade, I thought that it would be important to give them some kind of experience that would be a capstone to

their middle school years and serve as somewhat of a rite of
passage as they entered high school.

I remember watching MTV one evening and turning to Kristin,
"What if we did our own version of 'Road Rules' with these
graduating 8th graders?"

"Right, I am sure their parents would let us take them on a trip
in an RV."

But I was serious, so I grabbed a notebook and started writing
down my ideas. It looked something like this:

• 15-20 8th graders
• 4-5 adult leaders
• 3-4 RVs
• 1 week
• Fun activities
• Life Lessons
• Pack and prep our own meals
• "Mystery Trip" - kids won't know daily schedule

I shared the idea with Patrick, my boss at the church, and he
gave it the green light. We started recruiting kids, and within
just a couple of weeks, we had 22 8th graders signed up. I
asked three other young adults to join Kristin and me as
leaders. We rented four 7-passengers RVs, and started making
plans for where we would go and what activities we would do.
We printed "RV Trip" t-shirts for each kid, crafted a passable
liability waiver, and wrote packing lists for each participant.

Looking back, it was right on the edge of crazy, in so many
ways. It was 1999. I was 24 years old and Kristin was 25. The
other three "leaders" were even younger than we were! For

some reason, the parents of these middle schoolers trusted us to drive their kids around the mid Atlantic in 35-foot long motorhomes for a week!

Part of the plan included committing to eating only a few of our meals out at fast food restaurants during the trip, so each guy and girl on the trip brought specific food items that we would use to make all of our meals while we stayed at state park campgrounds.

The week was an amazing success. I planned a number of surprise activities, including tubing on a lake in Maryland, sliding down a natural rock waterslide, and staying at a sandy campground near the beach in Delaware.

The kids were split into groups for meal prep and clean up, and we gathered each evening for a meeting, where myself and the other leaders taught life lessons that we hoped would help with the transition from middle school to high school.

One of the highlights, for me specifically, happened about four days into the trip. We arrived at a campground at the very northern tip of the Chesapeake Bay at a place called Elk Neck State Park. After pulling the RVs into the sites and getting settled, we all made the short hike to the state park beach for a cookout and time to swim in the bay.

When we arrived at the pavilion near the water, we were happy to see that no one else was around. That meant that our group of 27 could be as loud and obnoxious as we wanted. It was a beautiful July evening, and the setting sun was slowly making its way to the horizon.

We grilled burgers and hot dogs, ripped open a few bags of chips, cut up a couple of watermelons, mixed together some lemonade, and had a big feast. After dinner was cleaned up, everyone headed to the water.

Because we were at the end of the bay, the water was glassy calm, so we tossed a frisbee around, played "chicken fights", and threw Drew, one of the smaller 8th graders, into the air and watched him do flips.

I remember thinking "This is beautiful. This is a picture of the simple joy of life in community and fellowship."

After about 15 minutes, I felt the need to take a few moments by myself. I left the students under the watchful eyes of the other leaders and swam away from the group, to a still and quiet spot in the lake.

Swimming a bit farther away, I took a moment to be alone and at peace. I dipped fully down under the water, feeling a chill come over my body.

As I emerged, I remember facing the sun, and feeling its bright rays hit my face. The light was shining at me and the air above the surface of the water was warm. Being the goofball that I am, submerged myself back underneath, holding my breath and allowing the chill of the cool water to cover me from head to toe. Then, facing the sun, I slowly rose, emerging only the top half of my head, feeling the warmth and opening my eyes to the bright light in front of me.

Just then, as if coming from outside of myself, I had a sensation of hearing God's voice. It wasn't in my ears, but rather in my spirit, or soul. It said, "This is heaven. Heaven, compared to what you experience in this earthly life, is like emerging from the breathless, dark, cold water, into warm, open, bright light."

I descended again, then rose slowly to feel the warmth and light of the sun, just allowing my nose to peek above the surface of the water to breathe in the evening air.

As quickly as the moment came, it passed. Mainly because I was interrupted by the voice of one of the middle school boys, Mike, yelling from across the water,

"Hey Mark, what are you doing over there, dropping a deuce?"

Middle school boys can always be counted on to say just the right thing at just the right time.

I turned and swam back over to the group, rejoining the fun as the sun continued to set across the bay.

We played more in the water, then headed to the campsites, where we gathered for our evening group meeting.

As I fell asleep that night, I thought about my sunset "encounter" and for just a moment, a sliver of doubt came into my mind. Was it really a holy moment, or just my vivid imagination getting the best of me? Was the thought of the sun shining on me a divine experience, or just wishful thinking?

The next morning, I was the first person to wake up. The moment I stepped out of the RV, I was standing in the middle of a steady rain. Our plans for the next day were to continue on to the Delaware coast for beachfront camping, so this rain was an unwelcome start to the day.

true stories

This was 1999. There was no way of simply taking out my iPhone and checking the forecast to see if the rain would last throughout the day, so I could only hope for the best and prepare for the worst.

As part of the plan for the trip, to keep things as simple as possible, we committed to only taking showers in the campground bathrooms, rather than trying to actually use the showers in the tiny RV bathrooms.

I gathered together my towel, toiletries, and clothes for the day and headed to the bathhouse as steady precipitation fell from the gray sky.

By the time I walked into the bathhouse, the doubt that I allowed to creep into my mind the night before had grown into full out denial. The moment in the water at sunset now seemed like a really corny thing, and I decided that I wasn't ever going to tell anyone about it.

I was pleasantly surprised to discover that this facility had hot water. I stood in the small shower stall and let the warm water clean off the grime from the last two days of travel and sharing an RV with a handful of smelly 8th graders.

Standing there, I looked up and noticed that the bathhouse had a series of rectangular windows along each wall, about 10 feet up on each side, to let in natural light. This morning, however, only cloudy, dark skies could be seen through the openings.

I closed my eyes as the water ran over my head and face. The weather reflected my mood, and I started to feel a sense of unexplainable dread settle over me.

With my eyes closed, something happened that I didn't expect. I felt a warmth come over my body, and realized that it was caused by the light of the sun. The sound of the rain on the tin roof of the building ceased and was replaced by a peaceful silence.

I opened my eyes, and there in front of me I saw a strangely familiar shape. The light of the sun was shining through one of the windows and onto my head, but just from the nose up. The outline of the shadow of this shape was thrown onto the wall of the shower stall, as bright as the light from the sunset from the previous evening.

The shape of my head, outlined on the wall, exactly matched the way the light from the sun was shining on my face from the previous evening's sunset.

My doubt and skepticism about my experience from the previous evening was immediately replaced with a sense of confirmation and clarity. Not only did I now embrace the experience as a true encounter with God, but I sensed very strongly that both of these moments were connected by an invisible thread, pointing to the care and presence of a loving God.

A rainy start to the day? The clouds rolling away, replaced by warm sunlight, shining in through the window of that bathhouse, at that exact moment? If the sun was just a little lower or a little higher in the sky, I wouldn't have known. If I was facing the other direction, I would not have seen the outlined shadow of my head. If I had even chosen one of the other shower stalls...nothing.

Me, exactly five feet nine and three quarters inches tall, standing there in that specific place at that precise time, with the exact same warmth of the sun shining on my head in the same way as it had twelve hours earlier? It still gives me chills. In my spirit, that still, small voice once again whispered, "Mark, it's me. Don't doubt."

This is one of those experiences that I look back on whenever I have intellectual doubts about God. Yes, there are times when I doubt. It's actually a natural part of faith. But I can't doubt that event. It happened. I became keenly aware of God's presence in a way that defies logic or reason.

There are many strange stories in the Hebrew Bible (what Christians call the Old Testament). Sometimes when we read them, they can be difficult to understand, because of the many cultural differences, as well as the way in which ancient people told and recorded events.

In one such narrative, a man named Jacob sets out on a journey to find a wife. There are many parts of the story that are confusing to anyone reading it today, again, because the cultural differences between the 21st century and when the story took place are vast.

In some ways, it's like trying to explain to you all of the facets and aspects of taking 22 8th graders on a week-long RV Trip. In a certain sense, the phrase "you had to be there" is very accurate.

But within Jacob's story there is an event that is told to help us each see what is really going on. After a long day of travel, he lies down to sleep, and has a very vivid dream. In the dream he perceives there to be a stairway (or gateway) to heaven.

Today, we'd call this experience a "lucid dream", so realistic that it seems to blur the line between dreaming and a lived experience. God appears and speaks to him, promising that he will have a family and land and blessing.

Jacob wakes up and says,
"Surely the Lord is in this place, and I was not aware of it."
Genesis 28:16

He went to bed not thinking about God, and woke up realizing that God was there.

That morning, during the RV Trip, standing in the shower, was my own version of that. I wasn't looking for it or anticipating it. In fact, just the opposite. Despite my lack of desire or hope or seeking, God broke through, and did so in a way that I clearly perceived and understood.

How many times in life do we miss out on the intersection between the divine and our daily experiences, simply because we aren't looking for such things to take place?

Exactly one year after the RV trip, I found myself in Juarez, Mexico with a group of high school students. We were working at a local church, helping to build a retaining wall that would serve as a foundation for an outdoor patio that they were adding to their church building.

It was a typical hot summer day, and we'd been working all morning to carry buckets of dirt to use for the project. Finally, along the horizon in the west, we saw serious storm clouds forming, and soon, cracks of lightning and thunder rippled through the sky.

true stories

Our group of 40 headed inside the small church chapel to take shelter from the incoming storm. We sat on the wooden benches, waiting for the storm to pass. One over-enthusiastic person in the group suggested that we use our break to spend time singing some churchy praise songs. Picking up his acoustic guitar, he headed to the front of the room and started playing his sequence of Christian chords.

Most of the group rose to their feet to sing. Not me. For whatever reason, I had a bad frame of mind about the whole thing.

Are you noticing a pattern here? "Church youth pastor with a bad attitude." Guilty as charged.

I stayed seated with my head down. Maybe it looked like I was praying, but I wasn't. I was checked out, tired and internally rolling my eyes.

The singing went on for another 20 minutes, with the sound of the rain continuing to rattle the metal roof of the small chapel.

Suddenly, it was quiet. As I sat in my spot towards the back of the room, I looked up to the small rectangular windows that lined both sides of the room. The storm had passed as quickly as it had arrived, and the sun was now shining brightly.

I looked down to my left, and on the ground, I saw a familiar shape, formed by the light of the sun as it shined through one of the windows: my head's shadow, from the nose up, framed against the ground, formed by the light of the sun shining in from one of those small windows.

The same shape from the RV Trip, exactly one year, to the day, from the previous experience. Then, looking down, I realized that I was wearing a specific t-shirt.   Right across my chest were the words "RV TRIP '99" - the shirt we'd made for the trip exactly one year prior.

I was once again overcome by the sense that God was present in the moment. All of the same circumstances: the place I was sitting in the room in relationship to the windows, the fact that I was sitting and not standing, the sun's position in the sky placing it exactly within the frame of the window, the fact that a thunderstorm preceded the moment, and, to top it off, the RV trip t-shirt.

My bad attitude was immediately replaced by the welling up of tears in my eyes. I knew that God was speaking to me again, letting me know that He was with me, even though I wasn't exactly making myself open or available.

"Surely the Lord is in this place, and I was not aware of it."

That day in Mexico, and the year before at Elk Neck State Park, were divine gifts. They were moments of encounter that for me were undeniable intersections of an eternal, all-knowing God with me, a finite, broken, human being.

Over the years, I have had so many other times that, in subtle and not-so-subtle ways, my life has been interrupted with these moments. I am still tempted to chalk them up to coincidence, but I choose to believe that it's something much more. That's not just true for me, but for every single person. Life is either a series of events that are leading to something beautiful and meaningful, or life is random, meaningless and hopeless.

true stories

It's up to each individual to choose how they perceive the events of their lives.

May you learn to see God and have an increasing awareness of His presence.

And may you learn to recognize through it all: the good, the bad, the celebrations and the losses, the joyful and the solemn, He is there, weaving together each moment into your one-of-a-kind **true story**.

true stories

thanks

I hope you enjoyed reading this book.

There are so many people that have been a part of my journey so far. Each person has played a part in helping me discover my gifts, find my place, and open up to genuine faith.

Obviously, there are many people mentioned in the chapters who have been great influences in my life and have impacted me over the years. And there are countless others who are not mentioned in this book who have also had a part to play in my journey. I am grateful for all of you!

This book was launched on Kickstarter with the backing of more than 100 amazing people, who each made a financial investment to help me produce a self-published product that (hopefully!) looks and feels professional.

I also am so grateful to family and friends who gave their time to help make this book the best possible version.

My aunt and uncle, Joni and Lou Heckler, provided feedback, guidance and encouragement. Their support and help not just with this book but over the course of my life has been invaluable.

Meredith O'Connor and Sandy McNamara not only supported the Kickstarter, but volunteered to review the first draft and provided helpful feedback and editing.

My parents have been an incredible example of what following Jesus looks like and have shown me consistent love and guidance over many years.

My four children have taught me so much over the years about myself and God and the great world that He created. I am blessed to be dad to Hannah, Haley, Jamir, and Braedan.

Finally, my amazing wife Kristin has been the constant thread of love and forgiveness and patience since we met at a college bar in the fall of 1995. She is the best person I know and my #1 example of humility, courage and resilience.

I'd love to hear about your story.

Feel free to reach out to me at 412-865-9015.

Mark